Keep It SuperSimple

tips from a recovering perfectionist

Bronwen Sciortino

Keep It Super Simple

tips from a recovering perfectionist

Bronwen Sciortino

© Copyright Bronwen Sciortino 2015

First Published in 2015 by sheIQ Life Pty Ltd.

All rights reserved. No part of this publication may be reproduced, stored in a retrieval system, or transmitted in any form or by any means, electronic, mechanical, photocopying, recording or otherwise, without the written permission of the publisher.

Illustrations: Dale Simmonds, Giant Advertising www.giantadvertising.com.au

Typesetting: Kelsey Allen, Media Highway www.mediahighway.com.au

Printed in Australia by Open Book Howden Pty Ltd www.openbookhowden.com.au

ISBN is 978-0-9943188-0-0
ePUB version: 978-0-9943188-1-7
PDF – Merchant version: 978-0-9943188-2-4

Sciortino, Bronwen

Keep It Super Simple (Tips from a Recovering Perfectionist)

ISBN is 978-0-9943188-0-0
ePUB version: 978-0-9943188-1-7
PDF – Merchant version: 978-0-9943188-2-4

ABOUT THE AUTHOR

Bronwen Sciortino is a recovering perfectionist who spent over 17 years as a high powered, award-winning executive in a soul crushing industry before developing the KISS principles and stepping away from a traditional life.

Working with people globally through corporate programs, conference platforms, retreats, one-on-one programs and in the online environment, Bronwen inspires individuals to simplify their lives and embrace the concept of an economy of enough.

Bronwen is passionate about working to achieve a goal of showing people there is a very different way of living life – driven by the power of lifting consciousness, waking people up and increasing self-awareness world-wide.

Bronwen believes in the positive impact that communities can have globally, and that the best is yet to come!

DEDICATION

This book is dedicated to my husband Jon.
You loved me when I didn't know who I was; you loved me no matter what.

Contents

CHAPTER 1	INTRODUCTION	1
CHAPTER 2	WHAT IF THEY'RE WRONG?	6
CHAPTER 3	ENOUGH IS ENOUGH!	16
CHAPTER 4	PERFECT	25
CHAPTER 5	SPIRALS AND CHOICES	35
CHAPTER 6	I AM	44
CHAPTER 7	CHANGE	53
CHAPTER 8	BUSY	63
CHAPTER 9	SETBACKS	71
CHAPTER 10	SENSE OF SELF	80
CHAPTER 11	LIFE BEGINS AT THE END OF YOUR COMFORT ZONE	90
CHAPTER 12	MAGIC	99
CHAPTER 13	NO IS A COMPLETE SENTENCE!	108
CHAPTER 14	CONCLUSION	117
	CONTACT DETAILS	119
	REFERENCES	120
	THANK YOU	121

Keep It Super Simple

CHAPTER 1

Introduction

My name is Bronwen and I am a recovering perfectionist.

My life imploded in the blink of an eye. In the space of an hour, I went from being an independent, highly functioning, award winning business woman to a puddle on the floor, unable to stop crying and unable to participate or function in everyday activities.

I had been told for eight years that I had a patch of psoriasis (a skin condition) on my left temple. Long story short – it wasn't psoriasis but was in fact a large skin cancer that needed to be removed or it would slowly eat away my face.

Fast forward to the surgery – everything went well. On the afternoon of the surgery I was sitting up in the bed in the ward laughing and joking with the surgeon about having 'cut the crap out of my life'. Arriving home later that afternoon with a massive bandage stapled to my head, I was straight back into work with my laptop like nothing had happened.

A few days later I went back to my surgeon for the post-operation check-up where they removed the bandages. My husband, Jon, was with me and saw the wound before I did. I knew from his face that it wasn't good, but nothing prepared me for the shock I was to receive when I looked in the mirror and saw a large chunk of my head was missing. My world changed in that instance and was never to be the same again.

That one glimpse in the mirror shattered my reality and, so it seemed at the time, shattered me into a million tiny pieces scattered all over the floor. I held it together until we got in the

car to come home and then the tears started. I remember thinking 'I'm a monster", over and over again. My whole life seemed to come crashing down and all my hopes and dreams for the future were over and done with. I didn't know where to turn, I didn't know what to do, and for the first time in my life I had no idea how I was going to 'fix' this situation.

You see, I was a 'fixer'. I'd always been able to sort problems out for others – it was one of my major strengths, or so I was told. If something was broken, someone had a problem, or someone needed advice about which way to turn, what to do or which way to go then I was the one they turned to. That's great, but none of that helped me in this situation.

From the moment I left the surgeon's offices I completely withdrew from everyone. I couldn't go anywhere, see anyone or talk to anyone. I retreated into my mind; into a dark and lonely place where the conversation was negative, hurtful and, at times, vicious and where all hope for the future was lost.

Apart from Jon, who was living in the same house, and a few brief phone conversations with my mother and sister who were living in different states, I talked to no one. I was completely oblivious to emails, phone calls, text messages, social media – any communication of any kind. I was totally lost to the world except for one phone call that penetrated the fog. My friend Anna called me to see how I was doing post-surgery and for some inexplicable reason I answered the phone. Within twenty-four hours of talking to me, Anna had sourced a place for me with a counsellor who specialised in working with cancer patients and so began the long and painful road of recovery to my new path in life.

This is my story, written as part of my recovery, but mostly because I wanted to share what I've learned so that others don't have to reach the breaking point that I did.

When you're in a million pieces, broken, on the floor and unable to stop crying it's really hard to work out which way to turn to get some relief. I was so afraid of change that I left making simple changes in my life to the point where change was forced on me by nature. My body and mind could no longer live in the environment I had imposed on them so they created a situation that forced me to change.

Through this process I've learned a lot about how we're made up as humans, and it's given me an opportunity to help others implement small, simple things into their daily lives that will help them to implement change on a regular basis, without the crisis that goes with it. And for those times in our lives when we do have a turning point that comes from crisis, hopefully implementing these small steps will help us to recover more quickly and transition seamlessly into our new path.

My journey has seen me develop a Keep It Super Simple (K.I.S.S) process that helps me to navigate the demands of everyday life. I've used this book to explore different areas of my life that I have struggled with and to share with you some of the solutions, tips and tricks I've come across to live my life in these areas in a different way. I've combined wisdom and simplicity to come up with these tools and now they've become my KISSdoms. Because I want to make this book a really simple tool to use, I've included a few KISSdoms at the end of every chapter to give you some ideas about how to get started in including KISSing in your life.

Our lives are so complex when simplicity will do. As children, we're taught what's right, wrong, acceptable and unacceptable by our families, friends, schools, communities and the world at large. Perhaps the biggest turning point in my recovery was when I heard someone voice the thought *'what if they're wrong?'*

It took me a long time during my recovery to be able to look at myself in the mirror. I was utterly appalled at the image looking back at me, but mostly I had lost all sense of who I was. Having cancer presented me with one of the greatest challenges of my life. Surviving cancer gave me the gift of an appreciation of the simple things, along with the courage to traverse a new road.

CHAPTER 2

"Do you remember who you were before the world told you who you should be?"

(Danielle LaPorte)

What If They're Wrong?

We're all socially conditioned from the time we're born. Social conditioning is the process of training individuals in a society to respond in a manner approved by that society in general and peer groups within that society. The training usually takes the form of direct and indirect rewards or punishment to move us towards adopting the behaviours and beliefs of our family and community.

In general terms, we're taught the 'right' and 'appropriate' social patterns with regards to nationalism, education, employment, entertainment, culture, religion, spirituality and family life. What we're not usually taught is that the 'right' and 'appropriate' social patterns differ vastly depending on the social structure within which we find ourselves. This means that what we are taught depends entirely on which family, community, state, country, school and so on we happen to be born into and raised within.

One of the biggest 'Ah-Ha' moments of my recovery was watching a video where Gregg Braden (a New York Times best-selling author and internationally renowned pioneer in bridging science, ancient wisdom and the real world) was being interviewed and hearing him ask the question *'What if they're wrong?'*.

This simple question opened the flood gates for me and allowed me to take a step back and get a different perspective on my struggle. It seemed I had spent my life feeling that I was 'wrong' or 'bad' because I simply didn't believe the things I had been socially conditioned to believe. I had lived my life in a state of internal struggle.

In advertently, by trying to be the person I was 'supposed' to be instead of just being who I am, I had added multiple layers of complexity to my life by trying to squash my beliefs into a format that matched the social conditioning I had received growing up.

This turning point made me realise that complexity had become a massive part of my life. I had added so many layers to every aspect of my life that everything had become a slog and I had lost sight of what was really important. It was time to work through the 'stuff' in my life to simplify things and make my life more free and enjoyable to live.

One of the most complicated parts of our lives can be the toxic relationships we have – either without realising that they're toxic or because we feel we have no choice but to have them in our lives. Toxic relationships aren't just with people. They can be with groups, workplaces, organisations, things, substances and habits.

For example, I was brought up in the Catholic system and attended a Catholic private school. I'm sure that everyone who has been brought up as one religion or another has felt a frustration at some time about something to do with their religion.

I was at odds with 'my' religion from the get-go.

There is no doubt that religion plays a large part in society world-wide, and every religion has its positives and negatives. There are definitely aspects of the Catholic religion that align with my values and beliefs: treat others as you would like to be treated yourself, do no harm to name a few. But there are definitely aspects that really don't sit well with me.

I don't even want to begin to count the number of times that I have uttered the words 'I am not worthy' whilst reciting the 'standard' words of a church service.

It pains me to think about the number of times that I really had to wrack my brains to try and find things that I had 'done wrong' so that I could be 'seen to' be repenting through the confession process.

Unfortunately for me, the aspects that didn't sit well with me outweighed the ones that did and the impact that this had on my life was to make trivial things like 'I snuck an extra lolly while Mum was out' seem like the worst act in the world. My experience was that I internalised the messaging of being 'evil' or a 'bad girl' so intensely that I over-compensated to the opposite extreme and became obsessed with being perfect. No one was ever as hard on me as I was on myself and I internalised massive doses of guilt, shame, perfectionism and constant failure at never meeting the expectations I put on myself.

Every family and society assigns roles to its members and each person plays a part in the whole system. Every influence in your conditioning plays a part in shaping who you become, how you interact and the way in which you move through life. The social conditioning we receive dictates explicitly the way we respond to the role that has been given to us.

There is usually no one thing in our lives that creates the persona we adopt when fulfilling our role – it's often a large range of things that we cobble together and internalise to create who we become. From a young age, for varying reasons, I learned to supress my emotions. Emotions were something that weren't to be shared with others, they were contained within and weren't shown on the outside. There are many factors that influenced my suppression of emotions, but one example was that when I was young I used to have an explosive temper and I was told that unless I learned to control it I wouldn't get anywhere in life. Having self-imposed the role of perfectionist, my reaction to that was to suppress my anger which meant I went through life feeling like a failure any time I felt any anger. Eventually I reached a point where I convinced myself that I no longer felt anger, but in reality I went about my days with the anger bubbling away under the surface.

Somewhere along the way, perhaps in my endeavours to be perfect, suppression of anger then morphed into suppression of all emotion – if there was no emotion to be seen, then there was nothing that could be used against me, or used by others to form a less than good impression of me. Fine in its own twisted way, right? But what it really meant was I could be watching a hilarious movie where others around me were laughing hysterically and I would have a completely blank face and feel nothing. I was totally unmoved by things around me – my life had become bland and soulless. More importantly, suppressing my emotions meant that no-one would get any hint from me that I was failing in my endeavours to be perfect – if I could successfully hide my emotions, perhaps I would be successful in fooling everyone around me that I was perfect as well.

We all take on different roles at different times in our lives. Sometimes the roles we take on are good and beneficial for us, but most of the roles I consistently took on were because others didn't step up when they should. For years I took on responsibilities for work that weren't mine to take.

In one job, I knew that I was paid significantly less than another person doing the same role, yet I constantly took over large sections of their work because our boss recognised that they weren't doing their job well. I wasn't offered any additional remuneration for this work, so effectively I did my work and half of their work and my colleague got paid tens of thousands of dollars more than me. I didn't utter a word.

In another job, I wasn't paid for months because the company was experiencing financial difficulties, but the Directors were all paid without fail. I constantly took on the role of martyr in my endeavour to appear perfect!

A complex conflict I uncovered was the revelation that I had been working in an industry for 17 years that was at complete loggerheads with my personal values system. I often found myself working in environments where the business I was working for had established partnerships with other businesses where there was a clash of values. It was my job to make the 'system' work.

I worked for large corporates who had a completely different agenda than the small businesses that were engaged with their systems, and I was the go-between whose job it was to 'make' the small businesses toe the line and change. When the values don't match, you're on a hiding to nothing but I slogged away nonetheless, always feeling like I was letting the team down because things didn't ever really work out the way they were supposed to.

Perhaps the biggest conflict for me was working in an environment that was based on false representations, false expectations and was full of a lot of false pretences. Recognising this clash and making the decision to move my life to a different path has resulted in my life becoming so much simpler.

Once everything in my day became about being able to undertake activities that supported my values, I experienced a massive shift in my thinking and I suddenly found that opportunities appeared out of nowhere and the creative flow of my life took an exponential turn.

Part of my journey – before and after surgery – has been recognising that my life has been made more complex by the existence of triangles. The drama triangle is a psychological and social model of human interaction first described by Stephen Karpman, M.D. Triangles are situations where there are three people locked in a battle of some sort that results in particular roles being played. Each person takes on a role of either a persecutor, a victim or a rescuer. The victim is always the party who assigns the roles. Usually, the victim approaches the rescuer with their problem; the rescuer then talks to the persecutor to try and act as a go-between to sort out the problem for the victim.

In different situations, you can take on different roles so at different times in your life you can experience being the persecutor, the victim and the rescuer.

In my life, I was most often the rescuer, but I have also been allocated the role of persecutor and victim as well. Until I learned that I could take myself out of the triangle and walk away from situations that were causing complexity in my life, I continued to give my power away to others.

For example, for years there were a couple of really difficult relationships in my life. These particular people always made me feel that I was the target of animosity and 'underground' hostility. But I didn't feel that I could say anything to them for fear of causing problems and for fear of the flow-on effect of problems that this could cause for others in my life. I was absolutely in the role of the victim – my head was fairly and squarely stuck in the mode of believing that what they were doing to me was unfair, and I totally blamed them for the person I became where they were involved.

The worse the situation got, the more the situation spiralled out of control. I gave them complete power over my feelings and my reactions by allowing them to dictate how I would respond to what happened.

I found myself complaining about this during an executive coaching training session and my executive coach told me bluntly that until I was prepared to take responsibility for my actions and emotions I could expect the situation to remain the same or get worse. Effectively – if I wanted to change some things, I needed to change some things.

> *Once I realised that I could take my power back and I could make all the decisions around how I was prepared to react, act and feel in these situations my life was changed forever.*

Often two parties become locked in a situation simply because both parties continue to behave in the same way. If neither party changes their behaviour, then the tension remains the same or escalates. I decided that it was within my power to change the way I approached the situation. It takes courage to do this because it's not possible to know the outcome of the change in behaviour until you've gone there, but I took a deep breath, put one foot in front of the other and took the step to break the deadlock.

I eventually came to the realisation that the only things in the situation I could control were my behaviour and my reactions. This simplified things for me and allowed me to keep it super simple by putting simple steps in place to move forwards. My decision didn't necessarily suit the other people, but that wasn't what was important – the most important thing was that I took control of myself and made changes that made my life easier. It wasn't easy, but I can wholeheartedly say that it was completely worth it because I am now completely removed from the emotion around their behaviour. I can now stand in my power and understand that their choices affect their lives and not mine.

 **KISSdoms**

1. Learn to ask yourself '*What if they're wrong?*'
    - Take a moment to think about the things in your life that don't quite fit with your thinking. Write them down.

    _____
    _____
    _____
    _____
    _____

    - Then ask yourself the question 'What if they're wrong?' Write down whatever answers come to your mind.

    _____
    _____
    _____
    _____
    _____

    - Take a moment to consider whether making changes in these areas will make a massive impact in your life'

    _____
    _____
    _____
    _____
    _____

    - If the answer is 'Yes', write down three simple things you can do to make a change.

    _____
    _____
    _____
    _____
    _____

- Take one step at a time to work towards implementing these three simple things.
  _____
  _____
  _____

2. Identify the areas of your life where there are triangles.
   - Write down the situations in your life where there are people looking to you to solve their problems for them.
     _____
     _____
     _____
     _____

   - Prioritise the list of triangles into the order of the most intrusive to the least intrusive.
     _____
     _____
     _____
     _____

   - Taking the first triangle on the list, write down three things you can do today to remove yourself from this triangle.
     _____
     _____
     _____
     _____

   - Once you're removed from the first triangle, cross it off the list and move on to the next item until you have removed them all.
     _____
     _____
     _____
     _____

Notes

CHAPTER 3

*"So many of us never, or rarely feel that we are enough.
We fill our lives with self-improvement as
though we're lacking in some primary way."*

(Sark)

Enough is Enough!

Until my surgery, I spent my life battling with 'enough'. Enough was my demon, my nemesis, the mountain in front of me at every turn. At every stage it beat me to the finish line – it didn't matter how well I had done, how successful I had become, how much of an impact I had made. 'Enough' always raised the stakes so that I wasn't quite good enough. Perfect was never, ever attained.

Ultimately, 'enough' was the underlying lynchpin of my perfectionism. When the bandages were first removed and I saw the chunk of my head missing for the first time, my ability to be perfect was shattered forever. There was no way I was ever going to be able to achieve perfection again with a massive hole in my head. The worst thing about this was that there was no way I was going to be able to hide the hole either.

Even while trying to encourage me about the future my surgeon was still saying that I would only be able to partially cover the wound with my head. My ability to pretend I was perfect to the outside world had been taken from me.

I lost all sense of self. My hair had been cut really short and a part of my hair had been shaved for the surgery. When I looked in the mirror I didn't recognise the person looking back at me. The shock I had received when the bandages were removed was significant enough to shift my perception of reality completely. I was totally and utterly lost and overwhelmed.

I had pushed myself to extremes in all aspects of my life trying to achieve perfectionism. When my world shattered and I was forced to stop, I discovered that I was physically and emotionally exhausted. My body was broken permanently in too many places with ankle, knee, back, shoulder and finger injuries. My energy was almost totally depleted and completely out of balance. It was no wonder my body and mind had conspired against the decades of punishment I had inflicted on them.

My recovery was driven by learning about the hard-core conditioning I had put in place and releasing myself from the bonds of the 'rules' I had imposed in my life. For me this meant shattering the pillars of 'I am not worthy' and 'I am not good enough' and replacing them with pillars of love and kindness.

This showed up in a lot of areas of my life. For example, exercise and sport had always played a massive part in my life. When I would to go to the gym I would push myself to the extreme to punish myself for not being fast enough, fit enough, strong enough, slim enough you get the picture. I got to the stage where I couldn't go for a walk without timing myself to see whether I had been faster than the last time I had completed the walk. All this did for me was deplete my already non-existent energy even further, and add extra injuries to an already significantly injured body. I was driven to be better. I was driven to be good enough. There wasn't one part of my life that wasn't being compared to something and being judged as falling short.

Something had to give, but in order to change I had to acknowledge that it was okay to have things in my life that were simply for enjoyment, that didn't need comparison but were mine simply because I wanted them and enjoyed them. Because exercise and movement were such a big part of my life, and I felt good when I included them, I made the decision that I wanted to keep them in my life. To do this I had to change my mindset significantly around why they were an important part of my life. To change my mindset I asked myself the following questions:

1. How does exercise make me feel?
2. How do I feel when I don't exercise?
3. What combination of exercise is best for me?

By asking these questions I was able to work out that when I exercise I feel better, I have more energy and I can concentrate for longer periods of time. I have also discovered that exercise is really important for me when I am having a fragile day. If I move I can better work with my emotions.

I am much more likely to be sluggish and find myself in a more negative mindset if I don't exercise. I am also much more likely to make less healthy food choices if I don't exercise. Exercise works for me.

Exercise makes me feel alive. The blood circulates through my system bringing oxygen to all my cells. This feeling increases my energy and gets my creative inspiration going. My body now carries so many injuries that high-impact exercise such as running, netball, tennis and so on are no longer really an option for me. I played around with different combinations of exercise until I found a combination that I can consistently maintain without getting injured and being unable to do anything for weeks on end. For me, that combination is a mixture of yoga, cycle classes, walking and outdoor cycling. The time of year will determine the mixture – when it's warmer I want to spend more time outside so I tend to do more of the outdoor activities.

Most importantly, I scan my body every day when I get up and make a decision on the day as to whether I will stick to the plan or change according to where I am at that day. I have totally removed all expectation and judgement from the equation. If I am really tired, or my body is too sore, then I will skip a day or two and do some gentle stretches on the floor instead. The old me would have viewed my body needing a break as weakness and I would have punished it for its imperfection. Kindness is now the underlying mantra for my exercise regime.

> "The greatest prison people live in, is the fear of what other people think" (anonymous).

I was terrified that people would find out that I wasn't perfect. I lived my life in constant fear of exposure. I drove myself beyond breaking point to prove that I was good enough but within, I always fell short.

My self-expectations of me were always significantly higher than those of others around me. I had lost sight of the simplicity of life. One of my favourite things to do was to go to the beach and have fish and chips whilst sitting on a blanket watching the sun set over the ocean - yet it was something I did maybe once every two or three years. Such a simple, inexpensive thing and yet I couldn't find time for it in my life. I forgot to stop and look at the incredible view that we drove past every morning and night on the way to and from work. The grind of pushing myself to be perfect took over. I wasn't good enough so I had no right to enjoy any of the little things in life.

Punishment became the rock that my life was built on. I was so hard on myself and I drove myself harder and harder to achieve more and to make up for all the failures to date. I looked after everyone else and took on everyone else's responsibilities-almost always to the detriment of myself. If I was challenged or asked why I wasn't looking after myself I could come up with a myriad of reasons. Not once did I realise that none of the reasons were valid – I was too enmeshed in the story I was telling.

I had created a life that was slowly killing me... from the inside out.

I remember sitting down with one of my friends about six months after my surgery and she told me that I had been handed a gift when I had my breakdown. I remember feeling astonished that she could think that having a crater in my head and having a breakdown was a gift.

> *With the benefit of time, I now understand that I have been given the ability to take control back in my life. It hasn't been easy – my life was completely out of control and I was sprinting down the wrong path. Cancer was the thing that brought me to a halt.*

That halt allowed me to take the time to open myself up to a whole new set of information. I began a new learning curve that has enabled me to completely change the way I live my life. New people came into my life and I had the time to learn from them. My cancer wasn't life threatening in the traditional sense, but it made me see that the way I had been living my life was.

There is a host of information that has been lost to western culture for centuries, and it is starting to re-emerge. Its focus is on turning our attention within ourselves in order to connect with the external environment. My cancer journey has allowed me the time to explore this information and be open to finding the answer to happiness, wholeness and control over our destiny that lies within us. Simplifying our thoughts will help us to simplify our actions. If we're kind to ourselves we're more likely to be kind to others. If we recognise that we have exactly enough for right here and right now we'll also accept that there is enough for everyone.

Let's quit the struggle against ourselves, and against others, and acknowledge that our lives are fulfilled through the simplicity of living.

KISSdoms

1. Write down those things (people, activities, hobbies and so on) that you love having in your life.

   _____
   _____
   _____
   _____
   _____
   _____

2. Once you've written them all down, place them in the order of most important to least important.

   _____
   _____
   _____
   _____
   _____
   _____

3. For each thing on your list, ask yourself 'How does this make me feel?'

   _____
   _____
   _____
   _____
   _____
   _____

4. Then for each item, write down how often you want it to be in your life (for example, you might want to exercise every day, you might want to each chocolate every day or you might want to travel twice a year - you get the idea.).

_____
_____
_____
_____
_____

5. Start with the first item on the list and write down three simple things you can do to bring that item into your life.

_____
_____
_____
_____
_____

Notes

CHAPTER 4

"There's nothing you need to do, be, have, get, change, practice or learn in order to be happy, loving and whole"

(Michael Neill)

Perfect

Webster's Dictionary defines perfectionism as a "… disposition to regard anything short of perfection as unacceptable; especially: the setting of unrealistically demanding goals accompanied by a disposition to regard failure to achieve them as unacceptable and a sign of personal worthlessness."

Wikipedia defines perfectionism as a "… personality trait characterised by a person's striving for flawlessness and setting excessively high performance standards, accompanied by overly critical self-evaluations and concerns regarding other's evaluations."

Essentially, perfectionism drives people to attempt to achieve an unattainable ideal – and I had it in spades. My life was structured around achieving perfection. Everything I did was done to the extreme in my attempt at being perfect. My pursuit of perfection saw me push too hard for too long and I unconsciously put my life on a collision course with a breakdown – and breakdown it did!

My perfectionism was fuelled by my lifelong battle with 'enough'. Being enough was something that I struggled with in every aspect of my life. I wasn't fit enough, slim enough, smart enough, good enough, kind enough, generous enough. You name it, and I wasn't enough of it.

When you overlay this with a harsh and highly active 'inner critic', I was on a hiding to nothing in being able to achieve perfectionism. In short, I had set myself up to fail by creating a life whose main goal was never going to be achievable, which then fed an inner voice with circumstance after circumstance that fuelled an attack on how bad, wrong, inadequate, worthless, guilty I was. Pick any negative quality, and my inner critic took pleasure in branding me with it.

It didn't matter what I achieved in my life, there was always something else that I could have done to make it better and the end result was never good enough. When I was in my early 30's, I was named as the winner of a Telstra Business Women's Award. Throughout the application process my inner critic completely negated the things I had achieved to the point where I felt I had no examples that were good enough to be worthy of an application. Luckily, my husband stepped in and convinced me that it wasn't ridiculous for me to enter the awards, and he also reminded me of all the things I had done that were worthy of being included in the application.

Being a perfectionist means that the peaks and troughs of life become mountain climbs. The rollercoaster effect is heightened to the extreme. After submitting the entry I remember feeling really depressed about having submitted an application because it was ridiculous to think that I could be considered for such a competition. When I was announced as the winner of the award I was happy for about 20 seconds. This then transformed into feeling terrified that someone would work out that I was a failure and that the judges had made a mistake. The room was full of the most incredibly talented people I had ever met, I hadn't prepared a speech and I felt totally inadequate when accepting the award.

We went to dinner that night for a friend's birthday and I was horrified to discover that her husband had organised for flowers to be presented to me in front of the whole restaurant. Such an amazing gesture was overshadowed by the guilt I felt for stealing her limelight and I felt as if I had ruined her birthday.

My inner critic constantly found ways to take incredible moments and completely trivialise them. It would also then add the cherry on top and find a way to add a layer of fear, guilt or shame to make sure I really felt the impact.

> *"Everything you want is on the other side of fear."* (George Addair)

Fear, quite simply, is an emotion. How we deal with fear, and indeed how much fear impacts our lives, comes down to our conditioning as a child. If we are brought up in a fearful environment, or by someone who is fearful of lots of things, then it is likely that we will have similar conditioning.

Throughout my life I have had an odd mixture of fear and fearlessness. Give me the opportunity to participate in any adrenalin-based sport and I will grasp it with both hands and run as fast as I can to participate in the activity. Jon is always shaking his head at me for my ability to go on the fastest, highest, scariest rollercoaster and laugh the whole ride. Sky diving from a plane, jet boating, abseiling – you name it, I love it. However, put me in a situation where someone might find out that I am not perfect, and fear becomes the greatest, immediate threat to my existence.

A big part of my recovery was acknowledging that perfectionism did not serve me well and then using this acknowledgement to move to a place of acceptance of all the parts of me.

When I first experienced my breakdown, I described it as feeling like I was shattered into a million pieces and I didn't know where to start to put myself back together again.

Part of my recovery process was acknowledging that I didn't have to pick up all of the pieces again if I didn't want to.

Guilt can play a massive role in how we respond to situations as they arise. How often do we find ourselves doing things we really didn't want to, simply because we'd feel really guilty if we didn't do them? We find ourselves being people we aren't, doing things we hate and behaving in ways that make us feel really bad - simply to keep others happy.

As children we're socially conditioned to what is right and wrong. One of the social conditionings used to mould us into the 'right' kind of person is the use of guilt. Guilt is one of the most powerful emotions and once it gets hold of you it's really hard to break the emotional connection it creates. One of the greatest learnings I received from my counselling was that as an adult I have the right, and the ability, to determine what is good for my life. As an adult, I can make the decisions around what I accept as right and wrong.

Early on in my recovery when things were still raw and I was really fragile, it took small things like dropping and breaking an inexpensive glass to send me spiralling into a flood of uncontrollable tears. It was around this time that someone I had previously been engaged in a toxic relationship with decided that they would try to come back into my life. Their approach to this was to send me a gift to 'aid me in my time of distress.'

Some may say that this was a thoughtful thing to do but to me it was like an attack when I was at my weakest. It also created a distressful dilemma for me. If I acknowledged the gift then I was opening the door to a toxic relationship that I had previously closed the door on and I wasn't in any state to deal with; but if I didn't acknowledge the gift then I was being rude. I was stuck and I didn't know what to do.

The solution: Keep it Super Simple! I learned to break the problem down into manageable chunks:

- My first step was to look at the gift and determine whether it could be separated from the 'negative baggage' that I felt was attached to it. In other words, the gift without its 'baggage' became 'good'.
- The next step was to determine if there was a way that the 'good' could be released into the world where it was detached from the 'baggage'.
- I chose to pass the 'good' in the gift on to my counsellor, who had other patients who could potentially benefit from the gift, and therefore the 'good'.

This process allowed me to be comfortable with acknowledging that I didn't want the 'stuff' that came with the gift, so I extracted the 'good' and sent it into the world to make a difference in someone else's life.

This allowed me to sit in my decision as an adult and not react to the conditioning that I had received as a child. Guilt be gone!

Because of our social conditioning it can be incredibly hard for us to make changes in our lives (there's a chapter later in the book about change and why it is so hard for us).

For me to eliminate perfectionism from my life, I had to move to a place where I was free from fear and guilt. I had to move to a platform of progress, not perfectionism.

By simplifying everything down into bite-sized pieces I was able to concentrate on just taking one step at a time. I would set myself three goals and would put no timeframe around when I had to achieve them by. Each day, I would assess how I was feeling and make a decision around what I would do that day. Sometimes this was as simple as acknowledging that I was feeling really tired and fragile and allowing myself a day of reading, meditation or watching TV. Other days, it might be journaling or baking that was needed. At the end of each day I would stop and mentally assess how I felt before closing the book on that day and moving forwards.

Of course this was tumultuous in the beginning, but it taught me to strip away the emotion and create simple, easy steps that blocked out all the noise. To go through a day without any judgement on whether or not you're doing the right thing - and without any guilt about doing something for yourself instead of what you think others expect from you - is one of the most freeing things I have ever done for myself.

I once saw a comment placed on Facebook that went along the lines of "if our friends talked to us the way we talk to ourselves, how long would we keep them around as our friends?" Reading this was one of those moments when you feel like you've been slapped across the face and you can suddenly see things differently. Acknowledging this comment allowed me to 'fire the mean girl within', and move to a place where I can more readily accept all the parts of myself as being enough.

I'm not perfect, I never will be and that's okay by me!

KISSdoms

1. Spend five minutes looking at yourself honestly and acknowledge the things about yourself that hold you back. Write them down as they come to you.

   _____
   _____
   _____
   _____
   _____
   _____

2. Have a look at each item on the list and determine whether achieving them is important to you. If it's not important, cross it off your list.

   _____
   _____
   _____
   _____
   _____
   _____

3. Put the remaining items on your list in order of importance.

   _____
   _____
   _____
   _____
   _____
   _____

4. Next to the remaining items on your list, write down whether it is holding you back because of the expectations you put on yourself, or whether you are held back out of fear of what others will think.

   _____
   _____
   _____
   _____
   _____
   _____

5. Starting with the first item on the list, write down three simple things you can do to change the way you feel about it, and/or can do to work towards achieving it.

   _____
   _____
   _____
   _____
   _____
   _____

Notes

CHAPTER 5

"One's philosophy is not best expressed in words; it is expressed in the choices one makes ... and the choices we make are ultimately our responsibility"

(Eleanor Roosevelt)

Spirals and Choices

There can come a time in our lives when we feel that everything is out of control and every time we turn around we're hit with something else. For me, that time came about a year after my surgery.

I'd been battling and fighting my way through life for years, but it really intensified off the back of a series of massive and significant blows.

Firstly, I'd had the cancer diagnosis. Then the removal of the tumour and the discovery that there were four different types of cancer in it. This was followed by the shock I suffered from the bandages being removed and my subsequent emotional breakdown. Then, the company for whom I had worked for ten years collapsed, meaning that there was no money to pay any of my entitlements (such as redundancy, annual leave, long service leave, salary and superannuation owing). The next blow was finding out that the insurance company I was insured through suddenly decided to cut off my Income Protection payments – with no warning and no real reason.

Spiral, spiral, spiral, spiral, spiral. Down, down, down, down, down. Smack, after smack, after smack. All of this came off the back of three of the hardest and most challenging years of my work life where my personal values clashed violently with the industry within which I was working.

During this time there were many instances where I was caught in a downward spiral, my energy was totally depleted and I was wondering how much more I could take before I didn't get up again. I often wondered when I would finally hit the bottom so something could change.

We can find ourselves caught in different spirals at different times in our lives. You might be in a spiral with a family member, or a spiral with your health, or a string of bad luck with things that go wrong with your house. Whatever the spiral, it has the potential to be all consuming and it can drag you to a place where there seems to be no way out – you are stuck and can't seem to change course.

Stuff happens in our lives. What we do about the 'stuff', and how we let the 'stuff' impact our lives defines what happens next. It may sound like a cliché, but it really isn't what happens to us, it's how we deal with it that guides where we go to next.

One of the things I discovered through my recovery was that the story I was telling was at odds with what was going on, on the inside. My story was one of being strong, calm under fire, understanding and supportive of those around me. If you look at the example of the work I was doing, my story was always one about how what we were doing was helping people, and delivering services in a way that focused on the clients. Whilst all this was true, inside I was struggling with working in an industry that was all about façade, soulless money and the cutthroat competition that goes into making it.

I often think that we are called upon very early in life to make a decision about what it is we want to do. We leave school at seventeen or eighteen years of age and have to make a decision about which path we want to walk down. The choice we make here can lead us to become so wrapped up in worrying about what other people think that we blindly wander down a path that doesn't suit us, and before long we find ourselves stuck and feel like we have no choice but to keep going.

Going through the spiral I experienced after my surgery was perhaps the most tumultuous time of my life, and the only way I made it through was to completely simplify everything down to just doing things one step at a time.

'right here, right now, do I choose to feel better or worse?'

There were days when I had no energy and it was all I could do to make it to the couch, sit down and cry. I felt completely fragile. I would cringe if the phone rang or if I received a new email for fear of what was coming next.

Suddenly, the thought popped into my head, seemingly out of nowhere, that I had resources available to me that could help shift me to a different head space. I grabbed my iPad and started playing the first video I found. The video was one by Esther and Jerry Hicks and suddenly the message in front of me was that I had two choices in every situation, in every minute of every day of my life. I could choose to feel better about the situation, or I could choose to feel worse about the situation.

I made the decision in that moment that I would make an effort to be more conscious with each situation in my life. When things happened I started to disassociate from the emotion, take a step back and take a moment to ask myself "right here, right now do I choose to feel better or worse?"

It is our connection to the emotion of a situation, event or person that makes our disengagement from them difficult. If we can disconnect from the emotion for even a few minutes it means we can be more conscious about where the emotion is coming from.

When we disconnect the emotion from the situation, we feel a sense of relief at the release from the grip it has over us. We have made the choice to feel better. This then gives us the ability to look the situation in the eye and work out why we're so connected to it.

- Is it because it's wrapped up in the story we tell?
- Is it because we can't disconnect from the person involved?
- Is it because we're afraid of what will happen to us, be done to us, be said about us?

If we can identify this, then we are one step closer to being able to remove this as a stress from our lives.

I believe one of the quickest, and easiest ways to break the connection that the emotion of a situation has over us is to create a physical movement of some kind. Any movement will help – stand up, shake your arms and legs, walk around your office, get a drink, go for a walk outside – any physical movement to change the energy in your body.

While any movement works, I am a big believer that turning on music and busting out a few moves can completely shift the energy in your body, and can often bring a different perspective to a situation.

Music has been associated with healing, both physically and emotionally, throughout history. We would all be aware that it figures prominently in religious ceremony but if we look further into history it can be seen in legends about ancient Greek gods (Apollo was the god who reigned over music), and ancient shamanic rituals. Music also appears in history with characters such as Aristotle and Plato, both of whom are understood to have prescribed music to individuals they were working with.

Music has long been seen as a prescription for fear and anxiety and also as a powerful tool to restore health and normalcy. If you've ever been to the gym and taken your 'tunes' with you, you'll know that a workout to music often gets you into a groove and helps you to remain engaged with the workout for longer. Similarly, if the music isn't the right music for you, then the workout suddenly seems less inspired. My husband has often commented on the fact that I have been 'bopping away' at the gym when I've been lost in the music.

The nature of the music will influence the physiological effect on your body. Pitch, tempo and melodic pattern all have an influence over music's effect on your mood and physical processes. For example, if you're stuck in an emotional attachment to something you probably don't want to get out your most mushy song of unrequited love – it may serve to make you feel worse!

Spirals can rule our lives so long as we let them. They're tricky little suckers and can creep into our lives without us being aware, but once we do identify them, two small steps can help us change direction and step off the spiral.

- Firstly, move! Find a song you really like and get your body moving to it – let it take you over for three, four or five minutes and change the energy in your body.
- And two – remember you always have two choices in EVERY situation – you can feel better, or you can feel worse – the choice is yours.

KISSdoms

1. Take a few moments to identify those areas of your life that seem to go on, and on, and on. The ones that you can't seem to get away from. It may be a situation, friends, family, arguments, work – you get the idea.

   _____
   _____
   _____
   _____
   _____
   _____
   _____

2. Move the items on the list into order of the most impact in your life to the least impact in your life.

   _____
   _____
   _____
   _____
   _____
   _____
   _____

3. Taking the first item on the list, write down three simple things you could do to change the way you think about or react to this thing.

   _____
   _____
   _____
   _____
   _____
   _____
   _____

4. Make a commitment to implement these three things every day until the emotional connection to the item on your list is broken.

_____
_____
_____
_____
_____
_____
_____
_____

Notes

CHAPTER 6

"'I AM' are two of the most powerful words we ever use, for what you put after them shapes our reality."

(Anonymous)

I AM

If you stop to think about it, everything we say has the potential to come to fruition in our life – especially if we repeat it often. *There's always a little truth behind every 'just kidding,' a little knowledge behind every 'I don't know,' a little emotion behind every 'I don't care,' and a little pain behind every it's okay'* (anonymous).

Mahatma Gandhi once said:
"Keep your thoughts positive because your thoughts become your words.
Keep your words positive because your words become your behaviour.
Keep your behaviour positive because your behaviour becomes your habits.
Keep your habits positive because your habits become your values.
Keep your values positive because your values become your destiny."

The language that we use is very powerful and it's perhaps the most ignored aspect of our daily lives. I'm not talking about whether or not you use 'naughty words', I'm talking about the words you use in your everyday life that are impacting on your world. I have heard it said that whilst the tongue has no bones, we should be careful of the words we use because we can easily break a heart (verybestquotes.com). Our words have the power to make or break us.

When we are running on auto-pilot we very rarely stop to take stock of what is happening in our lives. We're conditioned to accept that where we are, what we're doing, how we're doing it and what we're saying about it is exactly the way it's supposed to be.

I can't count the number of times I have said the words 'I can't do anything about it, it's just the way it is.' I was so stuck believing that everything that happened had to be positive that I had completely overlooked that how we behave, react and participate in any situation is completely within our control. We may not have a choice as to whether or not we have to be somewhere, but we can certainly control how we behave and act in that circumstance.

Similarly, I've learned that the way we speak to ourselves can be one of the most detrimental influences in our lives. There are a lot of things I find frustrating about social media (things like shoving drama, venting and political views down the throats of others) but I also love some aspects of it. When people put up quotes, pictures and passages of text that are inspiring and thought provoking it can help to shift my day into a different focus and a different energy.

As a recovering perfectionist I spent a lot of time listening to the 'mean girl' in my head, and trust me, she had plenty to say. She's been a constant companion throughout my life, and until I was conscious that she was there, I let her run rings around me and let her shape the way I behaved and lived in the world. I'd spill some water on the kitchen floor and she'd say things like 'you're such an idiot' or 'you're so useless.' I'd trip over something or stub a toe and she'd say things like 'you're such a klutz.' I'd be in a meeting and want to ask a question and she'd say things like 'that's a dumb question, don't ask that.'

The best thing about recognising that there's a mean girl in your head is that once you're aware that she's there you can't forget that you've learned she's there and it becomes much easier to recognise her when she speaks up. Now, I get to be my own devil's advocate. So when she says things like 'you're such an idiot' or 'what if you fail?' I can answer her with something like 'I'm so funny', or 'but what if I don't fail?' Being your own devil's advocate means you are in control of the impact of the thoughts. You are in control of whether or not you take the mean girl's story and make it your own or whether you choose to laugh at what she says and move forward in a different direction. Boys – I know you also have a 'mean girl' inside… although I'm sure you will find another way to describe her to one another!

Once I started to take notice of what my mean girl was saying to me, I also began to notice some of the things I was using as part of my story that perhaps didn't work for me anymore. For example, when people were telling me stories of horrible things that had happened to them in their life, I would say 'I feel for you.' I started to notice that by saying this I was transferring the pain that they were feeling to myself, and I was absolutely a sponge for their pain – I lapped it all up and took it on board to ease the suffering of others.

Now, I respond to these situations by saying 'what was that like for you?' It still gives the other person the opportunity to release their feelings, but they can do it in a way where I don't take on their pain. What a revelation this has been in my life. I've come to the realisation that I have enough of my own 'stuff' to carry around without taking on the burden of others as well.

We often think about stories as being things we're told as we're growing up.

They're about love, and fairy tales and usually have some theme that we're supposed to learn from, and they often form a part of our social conditioning. But did you know that story telling forms a large part of our everyday lives, and that we're all story tellers? Our stories are the things we tell people when they ask us questions about our lives. They are the answers that we give when someone asks us 'how are you?', or 'what have you been doing?' The way we answer these questions will determine the path we travel in this world.

The more emotion we attach to telling a story, the more attached we become to the story. The more attached to the story, the more we weave the story into our lives. The more we weave, the more our lives mirror the story.

Before we can blink, our lives have become what our words have foretold.

'Oh! What a tangled web we weave when first we practise to deceive'. This famous quote from Sir Walter Scott is usually associated with intentionally setting out to be deceptive, but when you stop to think about the power in our words, whether consciously or sub-consciously, I believe that it applies to all aspects of our lives.

Often we have a few precious seconds upon waking each morning before our inner critic starts flooding us with thoughts for the day. How cold is it? It's still dark. I don't want to get up. I can't believe I have to go to that meeting today. I'm so busy I don't have time to think. That person is such a pain. I'm so angry at so and so …. and it goes on, and on, and on ….. IF WE LET IT!

What if our day could start in a completely different way? What if we could immediately silence the mean girl within and make our first thought one of gratitude? I recently heard an interview with Louise Hay and she suggested making your first thought of each and every day one of thanks to your bed for providing you with comfort, warmth and a good night's sleep. Then move on to a thought of gratitude for all the opportunities that the day ahead will bring.

Often we wait for something to happen for us to be grateful and thankful, but we can become so caught up in our lives and being busy that we either don't notice when things come to us, or we are so caught up in the whirlwind that we don't take the time to stop and acknowledge them. If we start our day with a gratitude practice then we set our focus for the day and we're a lot more conscious of when the amazing things – big, medium and small – come to us throughout the day.

One of my aims is to teach people that they can be mindful and deliberate in the way they fashion their lives. Let's create a habit where the first five minutes of every morning sets our intention for the day. Let's deliberately and mindfully acknowledge the mean girl within each of us and then put in place a plan to counteract everything she says with something positive. Let's combat her tongue with quiet little giggles and deliberate, strong rebuttal. Let's take the time to be conscious of the words we're speaking, with the knowledge that every single word is full of power.

Cut out the noise and watch your life turn the most amazing corner. Find the simplicity in listening to yourself.

 **KISSdoms**

1. Stop and think about the stories you are telling in your life.

   _____
   _____
   _____
   _____
   _____
   _____
   _____

2. Write down the themes that recur through the stories you tell.

   _____
   _____
   _____
   _____
   _____
   _____
   _____

3. Next to each theme, mark whether it is positive or negative.

   _____
   _____
   _____
   _____
   _____
   _____
   _____

4. For those themes that are negative, ask yourself the question 'How can I change the story I am telling so that the theme becomes positive?'

_____
_____
_____
_____
_____
_____
_____

5. Write down three simple ways that the story can change for the emotion to change to a positive outlook.

_____
_____
_____
_____
_____
_____
_____

Notes

CHAPTER 7

*"Everyone thinks of changing the world,
but no one thinks of changing himself"*

(Leo Tolstoy)

Change

Change is defined by *"Dictionary.com"* as making '...the form, nature, content, future course, etc. of (something) different from what it is or from what it would be if left alone'.

It's only a short word, but the word change can instil a massive amount of fear in our hearts. We've been socially conditioned to behave in an acceptable manner, to think in an acceptable way and to undertake acceptable activities. Change contradicts this conditioning and therefore often holds a large amount of fear of the unknown for us.

Without knowing it, our social conditioning can program us to be completely averse to change. If we're taught to fear change, then when it occurs in our life it causes significant levels of stress and can cripple our ability to make decisions about the future. We can find ourselves accepting a status quo that is not good for us simply because we are unable to entertain the thought of change.

So why are we so scared of change? Why is it so hard for us to take the first step to implementing change in our lives, let alone stay the course and integrate the change? For most of us, it's because we don't understand what happens within us when change occurs.

During my recovery, I came across some work being done by a guy named Todd Herman who is a visionary and leader in the sporting world. His work focuses on 'helping players get out of their own way - so they can reach their true potential...'

Todd's work shows that there are specific biological changes that occur within ourselves when we attempt to make a change in our lives. Change affects us on a cellular level. When we try to make a change in our lives it creates a change to the way our cell receptors receive information, right down to the hormones that are created within us. You're probably aware that hormones can affect our emotional response as well, so it's easy then to see how emotions play a significant part in how we deal with change.

Todd's explanation of how it works goes something like this. Our cells are constantly receiving information and, based on this information, they constantly replicate themselves. Let's use the example of being highly stressed. In a stressful situation our cells are constantly receiving a cocktail of hormones such as cortisol and epinephrine. The cells are accustomed to receiving these hormones and are constantly replicating themselves based on the signals they receive from these hormones. If we were to then decide that we wanted to introduce relaxation into our day – that is introduce change – our cells would suddenly start receiving a different hormone cocktail containing dopamine and serotonin for example. Our cells would then start to vibrate to be able to receive the hormones differently and it is this vibration that causes the emotional release within our bodies. It is this vibration that can sometimes trip us up in our attempt to change because it doesn't necessarily feel good straight away and the emotions that the vibration causes don't feel 'normal' because it's not what our cells are used to receiving.

This is where self-sabotage and resistance start to come into play, because we start telling ourselves that it doesn't quite feel right and it is our own stories that we start to attach to the change that is happening. For example, you've decided to introduce a couple of new fitness workouts into your week. The first session is great, and the second session feels good, too, but by the time you reach the third session your body has started to hurt and your muscles ache a bit and you start telling a story about how that type of exercise 'doesn't work for you' or you're 'too old' to exercise like that anymore.

> *…it sometimes seems that the greatest change can occur almost at the time when you're ready to give up and quit.*

Over time, if you stick with the change you want to implement then you can change the receptors in your cells. The cell receptors will eventually become used to receiving the new cocktail of hormones and will settle into the new way of being. It is for this reason that it sometimes seems that the greatest change can occur almost at the time when you're ready to give up and quit. The cells have settled into their new pattern – you just weren't aware that you needed to stick it out long enough to let them reach acceptance of their new hormone cocktail.

Knowing these things and being prepared for the process can mean that we can relax into the change more readily than if we are unaware and try to fight the change process. If we can quit the mental struggle and let our bodies absorb the change without additional fight the change can implement itself within us much more quickly.

When I had my breakdown it was like I was shattered into a million pieces and I had no idea how to start to put myself back together. I was forced into a situation where change was necessary: I had pushed myself too far, for way too long and the decision to change was taken out of my hands. The experience of change for me was entirely traumatic because it was forced.

When I was trying to re-build myself I wasn't yet aware of the internal influence that change has at a biological level, and I spent a lot of time caught in the struggle that most of us experience through the change process.

As has happened throughout my life, the right people appeared at the right time to help guide me through the re-building process until I reached a point where I could forge ahead on my own.

People often asked me what processes I went through to get back on my feet and functioning completely in society again. I always tell them that it was a long and often painful process but I fully credit baking with saving my life! They think I'm joking. But seriously baking was where I found peace. It allowed me to activate my creativity and gave me a sense of purpose. Even though I had withdrawn from the world around me baking allowed me to share my love and stay connected. There were lots of people who received pies and cakes and chocolate creations who didn't see me at all in the first months of my recovery. Jon, would simply appear on their doorstep with my latest creation. The secret ingredient in all of my baking was my love.

Perhaps the hardest part of my recovery was that I looked really well. One of the things I concentrated on was making sure I ate really healthy food during my recovery. Everything I had read pointed towards the importance of providing good, balanced fuel for my body during a period of such intense emotional upheaval. I truly believe that this played an important part in my recovery. The problem was it also created an unforseen difficulty that I hadn't imagined could be a significant impact.

When you have a physical injury it's really easy to point to that injury and show everyone the progress of your recovery. When your injury is internal it is much more difficult for people to see your recovery. Because I looked so well – I was constantly being told that I was glowing with good health – it was really difficult for people to understand just how difficult my recovery was for me. Especially when they overlaid their knowledge of how 'strong' I was as a person – the strength and looking well just didn't add up in their minds to there being anything wrong with me.

Every journey to recovery from any type of illness or injury is a very personal one, but from my experience in recovering from a mental illness, I wholeheartedly believe that it can never be compared to another. Each journey has been triggered by a different event, has different causes and is then overlaid by the different experiences of the individual through their life.

I will forever more be truly conscious of what I say to people when they are facing tough or traumatic times in their lives, because my experience was that people were totally unaware of the impact of the things they said to me. Comments like 'you're only given the things in life you can handle', and 'what doesn't kill you makes you stronger', and my personal favourite 'I don't understand why bad things happen to good people' - are all comments that are said to give the *person saying them* comfort. There is nothing comforting about hearing these things when you are in the depths of a deep black hole that you feel like you are never going to get out of.

The other thing I found was that most people made up their minds about what had 'caused' my breakdown, and then went on to decide for me what the 'cure' to my illness was.

What I know is that my experience made me question every belief I had. I didn't know where to turn to and I felt totally lost, overwhelmed and as if I had no idea who I was anymore. The best decision I made was to seek counselling and get some help from a professional to guide me through the process of putting myself back together. This helped me to work out what basic things I needed each and every day to help me put one foot in front of the other and move forward.

It was a guiding hand that supported me through the toughest part of my life. It gave me strategies to simplify my communication with Jon, which meant that I could clearly articulate to him what I needed him to do to support me through my recovery. It helped me simplify every situation so that I could dip my toe in the water to test where I was at and then retreat when I needed to, or keep moving forward where it felt safe to do so. It gave me the courage to work out what I needed for my recovery and to ignore the expectations, opinions and demands of others during the process. This ultimately gave me the power to decide what the right thing for me was at each step along the way. When I had 'smacks' coming at me from every angle, it helped me to block out the noise and simply do what was best for my recovery.

One word came to me consistently and constantly during this process – SIMPLE.

> *"My life had become so complex without my even realising it and it was time to simplify it and get back to the basics."*

Perhaps one of the hardest parts of implementing change is the impact of the influences from people around you.

Often, the most pressure to keep the status quo comes from those around us. Remember, most people don't understand what happens internally when change occurs, and sometimes we can forget that when we decide to implement change in our lives we can inadvertently create change in someone else's life – and this change is one that they haven't decided to make.

Additionally, most families and peer groups have allocated us a role to play and when we make a decision to implement a change it can skew the delicate balance in these groups. When you take these things into consideration and look at the big picture it's easy to see why the people around us may not be wholly supportive of our wanting to make changes.

One of the things I learned through my counselling was the importance of deciding what my 'truth' was. By this, I mean making a decision about what it is I want and then committing to standing firmly by this. I learned to visualise a sword of truth, planting it firmly into the ground and then standing strongly beside it. What this enabled me to do was to keep my eye firmly fixed on my sword of truth when others were trying to find ways to sabotage my attempts to change. Sabotage is a strong word here, and I use it in the kindest of senses. I don't really believe that people deliberately set out to sabotage my efforts, or that they planned attacks on my progress to see me fail. If most people don't understand what happens biologically when change occurs, then it is also reasonable to see that most people don't understand that they engage in behaviour that sabotages someone else's change. What was important in the process was making sure that I was aware of my behaviour, emotions and reactions and that I kept working firmly towards my goals for change. That way I controlled the aspects I could control and I let go of the struggle around other people's behaviour.

It's most often found in association with Alcoholics Anonymous, but the Serenity Prayer comes to my mind regularly for how fitting it is in making our lives more simple:

"God grant me the serenity to accept the things I can't change, the courage to change the things I can, and the wisdom to know the difference".

KISSdoms

1. Take a moment to identify those areas of your life that you would like to change.

   _____
   _____
   _____
   _____
   _____

2. Write down what changes you would like to see.

   _____
   _____
   _____
   _____
   _____

3. For each item on your list, write down what you think will stop you from achieving those changes.

   _____
   _____
   _____
   _____

4. For each item on your list, write down what you think will help you to achieve those changes.

   _____
   _____
   _____
   _____

5. Place the list in the order of most important to you to least important to you.

   _____
   _____
   _____
   _____
   _____

6. For each item on the list, write down three simple things you can do every day to help you achieve the change.

   _____
   _____
   _____
   _____
   _____

7. Work through the list until every item is completed.

   _____
   _____
   _____
   _____
   _____

Notes

CHAPTER 8

*And every day, the world will drag
you by the hand, yelling,
'This is important!
And this is important!
And this is important!
You need to worry about this!
And this! And this!'*

"And each day, it's up to you to yank your hand back, put it on your heart and say, 'NO! This is what's important."

(Iain Thomas)

Busy

'*I'm so busy*'... it's become the pre-requisite for proving that your life is a success. We fill our lives with layer after layer of 'stuff' so that we can prove to everyone we're busy. Every second of every day must give us a story to tell about what we've done, where we've been and who we were with. If we don't have this, then what have we got?

Our lives are a competition amongst ourselves as to who is the busiest. Social media exacerbates this because where we are, what we're doing, who we're with - even what we're eating - is now placed in the public domain for immediate consumption.

When we were young, we used to write all our thoughts in our diary and we would be horrified if anyone read them. Now we put all our thoughts on social media platforms and are mortally wounded if no-one reads them. How many times have you been somewhere and you look around the room to see more than half the people with their heads in their phones 'checking in' to some form of social media letting the world know what they're up to? How many times have you been in this situation and been one of the people with their heads stuck in their phone?

We get out of bed in the morning and work really hard to polish our 'busy badges' until they shine. We proudly pin them to our lapel and then go out into the day to see what else we can add to our schedule that will make our badges gleam even brighter. We're totally consumed by the 'busy-off' we're caught in, but most of us aren't even conscious that we're competing

for the title. Sure we're tired, exhausted, and often run down, but we power through so that we can show how resilient and tough we are; after all, we're busier than others and we have to maintain this status.

It doesn't matter that we're totally overwhelmed by how much 'stuff' we add to our plates. We have a thousand balls in the air at one time and, if you're anything like me, our inner critics are devastatingly harsh if perchance we drop one. Often we don't realise we've taken on too much until something happens to bring us up short, or in my case, drops us completely from a great height with such force that we simply don't get up.

When was the last time you stopped to look at what you're actually busy with? When was the last time you stopped and questioned whether the information you're receiving is actually correct? What if being 'busy' is actually just a fad, and one that really doesn't serve you well? If you sat down and gave names to all the balls you have in the air right now, what would you say about them? Are they worthwhile activities? Do they enrich your life or are they just 'things' that you are doing? Are they things you want to be doing, or things you feel you have to do? If you could take your pick from the list, which ones would you choose?

> *...we don't stop to ask the questions we should ask – the ones that can really change our lives, change our direction and change the way we think and feel about things.*

Often, we're so caught up in the competition of being busy that we end up doing many things we don't want to do, and very few of the things that we love and that really enrich our lives. Worse still, we're so busy being caught up in the competition of being busy that we don't stop to ask the questions we should ask – the ones that can really change our lives, change our direction and change the way we think and feel about things.

When I was told that I had a cancerous tumour on my head I was too busy to take it in. I had work to do, problems to solve, people to look after, money to earn, places to go, people to see and the list goes on and on and on. Even after the surgery, I was so 'busy' that I was sitting at home that afternoon with my laptop answering emails and prioritising the next set of work that needed to be done. It wasn't until the bandages were removed post-surgery that I received a shock strong enough to flatten me and render me incapable of getting back up. It was severe enough that I was forced to look at my life and work out where I needed to implement some changes.

The benefit of hindsight is that it is full of wisdom that we can learn from. When I look back now, I can see that there were lots of opportunities I had to stop and question the direction my life was going, but I was too 'busy' to take notice. Every conversation with my Mum would end with her saying "take care of yourself and don't try to do too much" followed by my saying "Yes Mum" with that inflection of 'whatever' entwined. Of course, she was right (yes Mum, that is in writing and you have proof that I said you were right!!) and I was too 'busy' to listen.

I am told that great trauma offers us great opportunity for gratitude. When my internal system shut down and I was forced to stop, it gave me time to explore the things that had influenced my life. I was so fortunate to have access to an amazingly wise counsellor who taught me the importance of asking questions, viewing things from my perspective and of making my own decisions about how I felt about things - instead of operating on 'autopilot' and applying the social conditioning that had coloured my view of the world for so long.

For the first time in my life it didn't matter that I didn't have anywhere to go, anywhere to be, or anyone depending on me. For the first time in my life I wasn't busy. I had the opportunity to be completely still and rebuild myself from the ground up.

I learned that busy is a badge that was helping to kill me slowly and painfully.

I also learned that it was a badge that I could decide to put down. All the balls I had been juggling in the air had fallen to the ground and remained there, and a funny thing happened – the world continued around me and I survived!

I can tell you this, the hardest part was taking a step back and leaving the balls to sit on the ground. Making the decision to walk away and leave them behind was hard at the time, but came with such a sense of relief that I knew it was the right thing for me to do. I was so conditioned to my life needing to be hard ('life's not meant to be easy' and 'work hard and you'll get ahead' were two strong messages playing on repeat in my life) that I had forgotten what it felt like to have something that was the right fit for me. I struggled for quite some time with the temptation to go back and pick up those balls. I am proud to say that to this day I am still winning the battle and every day it becomes more comfortable to be doing something that is right for me.

Now I test everything in my life with the question 'how does this feel?' If it helps me to quit the struggle and brings a sense of relief then I know it's the right thing for me to do. If there's an ounce of struggle associated then I know I need to question what I can do to remove the struggle from my life.

This process means that I can stay conscious with what's happening in my life and make incremental changes along the way. I know that initial change can be rocky to start with, but once the first few steps are finished it's much easier to move forwards and enjoy my life.

 KISSdoms

1. Take a moment to write down all the things in your life that you are currently doing.

   _____
   _____
   _____
   _____

2. Next to each item on your list write the word 'Love', 'OK' or 'Dislike'.

   _____
   _____
   _____
   _____
   _____
   _____

3. Take a few moments to write down things that you don't currently do, but would LOVE to be doing.

   _____
   _____
   _____
   _____
   _____
   _____

4. For those items you've written 'Dislike' or 'OK' next to, take a few moments to write down why you have agreed to do them, whether they are essential and how soon you can finish these activities.

   _____
   _____
   _____
   _____

5. For those items you've written 'Love' next to, take a few moments to write down how often you do those things and whether you'd like to be doing more of them.

_____
_____
_____
_____
_____
_____

6. Looking at these lists, write down which activities you can get rid of and how quickly. Then using your 'would LOVE to do list' work out when you can replace activities from this list with ones from the list of activities that are going to be removed.

_____
_____
_____
_____
_____
_____

7. Be brave – saying no is the first step in moving away from things we really don't want in our lives!

_____
_____
_____
_____
_____
_____

Notes

CHAPTER 9

"Life is a series of experiences, each one of which makes us bigger, even though sometimes it is hard to realise this. For the world was built to develop character, and we must learn that the setbacks and grieves which we endure help us in our marching onward"

(Henry Ford)

Setbacks

Through every adversity, we experience a form of chaos. For me, the chaos was total overwhelm, identity issues following the trauma of diagnosis, the visual affect following removal of bandages, and loss of interest in everyday life and social gatherings. This chaos resulted in a complete withdrawal from the world, family and friends, and a physical reaction of insomnia and tears, tears and more tears.

At the time, it felt like my whole life had been wrenched from me in a matter of seconds. What seemed like a well-mapped path suddenly seemed to have disappeared. It felt like I had lost the ability to think rationally, that my intelligence had evaporated and that my whole life was now a failure. I was well and truly stuck in a downward spiral and there was no getting off it anytime soon!

> *People assume that I recovered from all this because I am a 'strong' person. In truth, I recovered from this because someone taught me how to make things simple again.*

That's a lot to recover from and I would have to say it's easily the hardest thing I've ever done in my life. People assume that I recovered from all this because I am a 'strong' person. In truth, I recovered from this because someone taught me how to make things simple again. Once you simplify a situation it becomes a lot easier to take one step at a time.

Focusing on one step at a time is a whole lot less overwhelming than looking at the big picture and feeling the anxiety within you rise and take over your whole body. And the best thing about taking one step at a time is that you can choose how big the step is, and even whether the step is forwards or backwards. A big lesson to learn is that you can 'dip your toe' in the water to test how it feels and then take it out again if it's not really comfortable for you. Acknowledging that you can always put your toe back in the water at any time makes dipping your toe a lot less stressful.

In moving through any chaos there will always be things that unsettle and challenge you before you get to where you are going. These setbacks are part of realigning and readjusting yourself to move more readily towards your goal. In the harshest parts of my recovery it seemed that some of my setbacks derailed me completely. I would take a deep breath, put one foot in front of the other and take a big step and I would feel okay about the step I had taken. Then something would happen that would sideswipe me and I would feel that I'd been swept further backwards than where I was when I took the step.

I survived these setbacks purely and simply because I had a mantra that I chanted in my head. *'One day at a time, one step at a time'*. Yes, I felt the impact of 'things' happening in my life at a much higher intensity than previously, and yes, they continued to hit me at a very fragile time in my life. I probably felt everything tenfold because I was in a much more heightened sensory state, but breaking everything down into small pieces meant that all I had to focus on was taking one step at a time.

I removed any thoughts about where I wanted to be at a specific date or time, and simply focused on what my next step was. This meant that the focus became taking the step, rather than how quickly or slowly I took the step. When I removed expectation from the equation it became a lot easier to gather the courage to take the step. I generally had three simple goals written down at any one time, each goal being one step to take. I focused on the first step first, and simply took the time it took me to take that step. Once that step was taken, I moved to the second step on my goal list and then the third step. Once they were all achieved, I wrote the next set of three goals and focused on achieving those. My first set of goals was to:

1) Take care of the wound on my head daily.
2) Move at least five days a week.
3) Focus on eating healthy food.

These were very simple goals that allowed me to focus, that only needed me to take one step at a time and that I could dip my toe in the water and take it back out again until it felt okay.

Removing expectation from the mix meant that I could focus on the simplicity of taking one step at a time. Without expectation around how quickly I completed each goal, how well I had completed the goal, what others thought about how I had completed the goal, and even what others thought about the worthiness of the goal in the first place, I created a process for myself that was all about consistently showing up and putting one foot in front of the other.

For someone like me with a deeply ingrained belief that I wasn't 'enough' this new environment was a revelation that life can be lived in a very different way. The consistency of Keep It Super Simple, one step at a time, no matter whether the step was big or small, forward, backward or sideways meant that I created a space where I could grow and recover without pressure and judgement. 'Enough' is something I still battle with, although I have more peace with it now because I have experienced a different way of life. I've learned that it's far more kind to me to be consistent and that one step at a time is a simpler, more gentle way of life.

When your life is in turmoil it's easy to forget that there are countless resources available to help shift your thinking in a slightly different way. Sometimes all it takes is a small shift in the way you see things for you to break the struggle of a situation and move forwards.

Resources can come in the form of people, books, movies, emails, text messages, nature, songs and dance, just to name a few. I count myself incredibly lucky to have the most abundant supply of resources in my life. There are times when it seems that no matter where I turn I am handed yet another resource that will help me fulfil my destiny. There have also been times when I have been stuck in a downward spiral and I've felt so terrible that I haven't been able to stop and recognise the resource that will help me shift beyond the chaos.

For years I completely shut down my emotions and, in particular, suppressed anything that was remotely negative. For me to be stuck in a downward spiral of any kind was particularly cruel because it meant that I forced myself to suppress my emotion even further to be able to maintain an impassive exterior. In the absolute depths of the chaos after my surgery it was the wise words of one or two people that would show me a glimmer of light and focus my attention in the direction of my resources. I believe that we're always shown the way to the resources we need - whether or not we listen when we're told is entirely up to us.

Movement is such an important part of our lives. Finding out what works for you is the first step in setting yourself up to consistently look after yourself. For me, I know that if I don't move I won't feel good, so I try to include some sort of exercise or movement at least five or six days a week. This may be a walk in the water at the beach, a yoga session, a pilates class or a cycle class at the gym – I like to mix it up so that I am looking after my need to move without exhausting my body in the process. For some people, running every day is the thing that gives their body the energy it needs, while for others it's going for a walk or dancing every day. Everybody is different, so you need to find what works for you.

It's really easy to find yourself immersed in a downward spiral. We get taken over by the feelings and emotions that course through our bodies. We're attached to the story about how 'unfair' it is, or how 'mean' they're being. The whole situation makes us feel... well, bad! So why is it that we cling to this as if our lives depend on it?

It's important to work out how you feel about different situations, people, music, things, food and so on. For example, there were particular songs that would come on the radio or TV that I had to turn off because I would be in floods of tears hearing them. I couldn't have them in my world at that point in time. As I've recovered, those songs don't have as big an impact anymore. There are certain foods where, if I eat too much of it, my body feels slow and sluggish (for example, wheat). When this happens I know to cut those foods out for a couple of days to give my system a chance to reset itself and then I try to consciously cut back on them and replace them with things that give me energy. I've found over time that I reach for those things less and less, because I really don't feel well afterwards.

As one of the ways to simplify my life, I've implemented a process of determining the things that provide me with relief. Every morning when I wake up, I start the day with an attitude of gratitude. I am thankful for the warm and comfortable bed. I am grateful for the love and warmth that my husband Jon and my cat Stella give to me, and I am grateful for all the opportunities that the day will bring.

In any situation where there is conflict or discomfort or where I just don't feel good about it, I try to remind myself to stop and ask the question *'how can I feel better about this?'* Invariably, when I take the time to ask this question I can always find a way to change what I am doing to make things better.

If all else fails, my recommendation is to crank some tunes and get your body moving to music. Put on a tune that gets your feet tapping and your head nodding and maybe even gets you humming or singing along and I defy you to not feel better! Music affects us on a cellular level and can change the energy in our bodies. You don't even have to have actual music to turn on – all of us have the ability to play a song in our heads – use this when you need to shift yourself out of a funk!

 KISSdoms

1. Take a few moments out of every day to acknowledge those areas of your day where you have experienced a setback. It may be a big setback, it may be a small setback or you may have had a setback free day!

   _____
   _____
   _____
   _____
   _____
   _____
   _____

2. Acknowledge that the setback has occurred.

   _____
   _____
   _____
   _____
   _____
   _____

3. Ask yourself *'How can I feel better about this?'*

   _____
   _____
   _____
   _____
   _____
   _____
   _____

4. By answering this question you can find your next step forward and find the way that helps you change what you are doing.

_____
_____
_____
_____
_____
_____
_____
_____
_____
_____

Notes

CHAPTER 10

"Perceiving your own voice means perceiving your true self or nature. When you and the sound become one, you don't hear the sound; you are the sound"

(Seung Sahn)

Sense of Self

Most of us can go our entire lives without being conscious – almost as if we are sleep walking. Without even knowing it, we can be programmed to the extent that we allow others to tell us how to think, how to feel and how to react, and we respond to our conditioning on 'autopilot'. It's often less painful and more acceptable to others when we toe this line.

From birth to around the age of seven, our sense of self is acutely moulded by what is found to be acceptable by those around us. From the age of seven onwards we assimilate with those around us, having previously been moulded and shaped. Often we have learned our greatest lessons from punishment, disapproval, ostracism and other 'uncomfortable' experiences in our lives. We know what it feels like to have our ability to 'belong' to our community threatened, so we repress those aspects of our character that are deemed less than acceptable and we assimilate.

Over the years a whole industry has evolved around researching what makes individuals in different socio-economic groups tick. This billion dollar industry constantly conducts research to create programs that will hit our buttons and make us respond in a particular way.

This research can be used in a variety of different aspects of our lives and can program us to behave in a specific way - if we let it. Religion, schools, governments, military, private organisations - all can access this research at different levels to provide information to us in certain ways that make us respond in the manner they want us to. If we're completely oblivious to this we can spend our lives virtually sleep walking and acting in a programmed way.

For example, did you know that shopping centres can influence the way in which you shop simply by altering the colour of the lights in the passageways and the music that is playing? Have you ever noticed that your local supermarket plays different types of music at different times of the day? When it's really quiet the music is more likely to be cruisey, comforting music encouraging you to take your time and meander around the store. But when it's really busy it's likely to be fast paced and more adrenalin charged to encourage you to get in and out as quickly as possible.

Another example is the millions of dollars of research conducted every year by the manufacturers of slot or poker machines to test which sounds and flashing colours make you put more money into their machines.

There are highly researched sales processes in play in almost every store you go into – and in fact, now even in online situations – that are designed to not only make you buy, but more often than not to make you purchase something much more expensive than you had intended to buy in the first place – and all so you don't miss out on a deal that is too good to refuse!

Intuition can play a big part in our lives, if we just take the time to pay it some attention.

Our gut instinct is the way we feel within our bodies when our intuition is in play. Personally, I literally feel my gut instinct in my stomach – I get a wrenching, twisting feeling when something is happening that isn't quite right and I get a fluttering feeling when things feel great. Others tell me that they feel it in their toes, or their knees and I am sure others again feel it in different places on their bodies.

It's not really important where it's felt, the important thing is to become tuned-in to the feelings so that you are aware of what's going on around you. When we're conscious of our thoughts and their connection to our feelings, we can avoid the things that aren't quite right in our lives.

For example, I once received a phone call offering me the opportunity to buy four places on a cruise in the US for around $1,250, including airfares, accommodation and the cruise. The sales process around this was so slick that even though I felt my stomach wrenching and twisting I still went ahead and made the purchase. I must have realised at some point that it wasn't the right thing for me because during the phone call I said to the sales person on the phone that I didn't want to go ahead. They turned my 'No' into a 'Yes' by selling me on the concept of '…did I realise that I was going to miss out?' and their concern that everyone else was going ahead with the purchase.

I felt sick the whole time I was talking to this sales person, and on some level I knew I wasn't happy about making the purchase, but I did it anyway. To put this in context, I knew it was wrong – my gut instinct was screaming at me - and I get highly seasick, so even if my gut instinct wasn't screaming at me, why would I be buying a cruise package? Half an hour later I received a phone call from my bank asking me to confirm a transaction on my credit card. In discussions with them I found that there were a number of others who had been sucked into the same sales process, and the bank encouraged me to cancel my credit card and have a new one issued.

I've never forgotten how this felt. I was so embarrassed when I was talking to the bank - I felt like a silly little school girl that needed rescuing. I got lost in the emotion of the situation and swore to myself that I would never let those feelings be ignored again.

To simplify, essentially our gut instinct tells us whether the activity, situation, person is right for us. It's up to us to be self-aware enough to identify the gut instinct when it occurs, but identifying it isn't actually the hard part. The hardest part is being able to say 'No' to that situation, person or activity and to remove it from our lives. We know it's bad for us, our gut instinct has told us so, but we still do it anyway – why? Saying 'No' can often be more painful for us than walking away from the situation.

Perhaps the biggest question to answer here is whether self-awareness is actually all it's cracked up to be. Like most things that are worth having in life, self-awareness is great as long as you balance the good and the not-so-good aspects of it.

Self-awareness offers you the ability to understand how you are programmed, decide who you want to be, how you want to react and how you want to live your life. When used to help us be conscious of what is going on around us and of the messages we're receiving, and allowing us to live in a space that questions our world, self-awareness can accelerate our lives and urge us towards a life of happiness, content and fulfilment. But the dark side of self-awareness is that it can bring to our lives a process of identifying our actions, reactions and inner thoughts that we can then use to critically and obsessively punish ourselves for not being a better person.

Traditional, mainstream religion doesn't like to encourage us to be too self-aware because it can lessen the hold that the doctrine of its teachings has on us. My experience has taught me to be open to information coming from all different sources in our lives. There is good in every source of information – I see my job as filtering the information to take the pieces that serve me in my life, and releasing the pieces that don't serve me as well.

Our lives are enhanced and broadened when we approach situations with an open mind. Every one of us has the right to decide what the guiding light in our lives is. Nowhere is it written that your life will stop if you don't adopt every last piece of information from one source.

As humans we're conditioned to rely on community to survive, but what happens when the way we live creates a fissure in the way that community operates? More and more we're seeing reports from around the globe about individuals who go into populated places and embark on a killing spree. There is no doubt that these are cries for help; my question is whether the cries would have been heard earlier, or indeed would even have been necessary, if our participation in the community wasn't so removed from our everyday lives.

I'm talking about the global impact that technology is having in our lives. Technology can be great, and amazing advances are made every day that can save lives, improve communication globally and make our lives easier and more efficient.

But technology has also made us busier than ever before and added a layer of complexity to our lives that serves to disconnect us.

We're now connected and in 'contact' 24/7 – there are very few places in the world where we can't be found and where people can't contact us in one form or another.

Growing up I spent a lot of time outside playing, whether it was with the other kids in our neighbourhood, riding bikes, riding horses or playing sport. We worked out where our friends were by wandering to their house and finding out whether they were home, or picking up the phone and calling them. Nowadays, it's a text message or a message on Facebook that gives us this information – we're one step removed from the conversation.

We can see massive changes in the way that communication occurs now with the advent of social media, the use of text messaging, emails and online news, weather and communication channels. In one way I love that it is so easy to keep in touch with family and friends who live in completely different parts of the country and indeed in different parts of the world. It means that I can participate in their lives without actually being in the same place as them – it feels like I miss out on less of their lives and it enriches my life through being able to participate in theirs.

By the same token, it can also mean that I participate via technology in the lives of those who live close by – it's so convenient to send a ten second text message rather than spending five or ten minutes on a phone call, or dropping by their house for a quick chat. The result is that we're one step removed from the personal.

The way businesses communicate with us has also completely changed. Gone are the days when the only way to advertise was on TV, in the newspaper or in a magazine – now it's a text message, an email or a Facebook post that is received as well. Gone are the days where we have to go to a store to buy the things we want. Now we don't even have to leave the comfort of our homes (and in some instances the comfort of our couch!) to purchase the things we want. We're one step removed from the experience.

Technology means that there is now an avenue for individuals to openly have their say about others publicly and loudly – to the world at large. Whilst this opens an avenue for giving the little guy a voice, one thing I really don't like about the technological advances is the way in which individuals are prepared to make personal and vicious comments about other individuals they haven't met. Technology has opened up individuals to public comment in a way that has never been seen or experienced before, and in a manner that can spread rapidly through the use of social media.

In the 'old days' information was spread through TV, newspapers, magazines, newsletters and the good old grapevine. Information used to be controlled through one or two people in specific positions in an organisation and was generally checked for accuracy before being published. With the advent of online and social media there is now little to no emphasis on making sure the information is unbiased or even correct – it's all about being first to market and having a sensational headline.

Social media is often based on individual opinions, which are often uninformed, and based on an attitude of 'it's not fair to me'. The problem is that most of us have been brought up to believe in journalistic integrity and the unbiased nature of reporting facts to keep us informed and we're still in the mode of believing what we see reported by the media. We've not taken the time to stop and acknowledge that the way information is now provided to us has changed, and that very little of what is reported is actually correct or the full story. To me, it seems that information floating in the public domain has moved to a space of personal attacks, sensational headlines and comes from a highly negative place. We are often one step removed from the truth.

> *The greater good will no longer exist, and if that happens we might as well become machines.*

I believe it's so important for us to program time without technological connection into our lives. We need a break from the computer, phone, internet, social media - and we need to take the time to reconnect with our family, friends and community. We must bring the personal connection back into our lives to ensure that we continue to feel for our fellow human beings.

Without this personal connection our society will become totally and emotionally disconnected, and the decisions we make as a community will be disjointed and will serve only a small portion of our interests. The greater good will no longer exist, and if that happens we might as well become machines.

 KISSdoms

1. Take half an hour away from technological gadgets (I promise you will survive without your smart phone for 30 minutes).

   _____
   _____
   _____
   _____
   _____
   _____
   _____

2. Write down three things that have happened during the day that have made you feel more connected to your community.

   _____
   _____
   _____
   _____
   _____
   _____
   _____

3. Write down three simple things you want to do the following day to deepen your connection with your community.

   _____
   _____
   _____
   _____
   _____
   _____
   _____

4. As you get used to time without your technological connection, try to extend the period of time away from them so that you deepen your experience and connection with the world around you.

_____
_____
_____
_____
_____
_____
_____

Notes

CHAPTER 11

"My dear,

Life begins at the end of your comfort zone.

For tell me where can life be found in the normal? The unordinary?

No, life – true life, begins when you step over the edge. It starts when you take a leap of faith off the mountain of certainty (into uncertainty), and doesn't end until you're comfortable again.

Burst that safe bubble you call your comfort zone, and be uncomfortable – start living.

*Falsely yours,
Neale Donald Walsch"*

Life Begins at the End of Your Comfort Zone

My husband was reading me an email that had been sent by one of his work colleagues, who was talking about the process by which people suddenly 'get it' when he's trying to explain something to them. He described it as '…once you see it, it will be forehead slap city'. The minute I heard this I loved it. It completely encapsulated what happens to me when I receive information that seems to be so simple, so obvious; so right – and yet I've been completely oblivious to it for so long.

My life was passing me by and I had no idea. I spent over 17 years slogging away in an industry that crushed my soul, and I had no idea. One of my greatest 'forehead slap city' moments came when I realised that I had continued to do the same things in life, day after day, while expecting and hoping for a different outcome. I was well and truly in my comfort zone. But then I started questioning all the different things in my life and I was left wondering whether it was actually a comfort zone or whether I was actually in a massive 'rut'. How can you tell the difference? It seemed to me that the two were alarmingly similar in their traits.

Possibly the worst part of this revelation was realising that I had become something that drove me crazy in others. I had become a 'gunna'. I was telling myself and others all sorts of stories about the things that I was going to do (is 'gunna' do). I had been doing it for years. Talking about my dreams of having my own business and working with others to help them understand their finances better.

In fact, I had become so enmeshed in my comfort zone that I hadn't even realised that my dreams had their feet planted firmly there! I had become totally insular in my thinking. I was stuck in a rut, and wasn't even remotely looking around for the possibility that life might have so much more to offer me.

These questions put me on the path of trying to understand why I did the same things day in day out despite the fact that they were slowly killing me. So, I started to evaluate my life. I critically assessed whether I was doing things on 'autopilot' or whether I was consciously making the decision to do something differently. Are you surprised to hear that 99% of everything I did was on 'autopilot'? I was. I thought I was so evolved, that I was spiritually awakened, highly conscious and operating at a high level.

What I discovered was that whilst I had some skills in consciousness, I was actually using them to fuel my perfectionism. I had turned being conscious into being even more highly critical of myself, and then I berated myself even further for not being perfect – after all, I was so conscious, so aware and I was still failing. The outcome? I had sunk even further into my comfort zone.

So why do we stay in the same day-to-day choices, living the same day-to-day life without making any changes? I pondered this question a lot during my recovery and the only answer I came up with was that there is a different answer for all of us. For me, it was about being perfect. I went to the extreme to have the right education, the right job, the right attitude, the right demeanour, the right answers, ad infinitum. I was convinced that challenging myself and doing something that might feel uncomfortable might send the wrong message to people and they might lose their perception of me as being successful and a high achiever.

I was entrenched in 'playing the game'. The only problem was, I had made up the game, it was focused around perfection and it was impossible for me to ever win.

> *I had no idea that I had the power to obliterate the game by simply making the choice not to play anymore, or to change the rules, or to change the purpose of the game, or even to start playing a completely different game altogether. The choice was always mine –*
> *I had hidden from any information that led me to making it.*

In one way I was lucky - my emotional collapse made me incapable of doing anything. Nothing in my life was as it had been and I could do nothing except cry. You could say that I had forced myself into a situation where I was no longer capable of playing the game, so it automatically came to a halt. The challenge for me from this point forward was to realise that I had set up my game in a way that was at odds with what I wanted from my life. In order to move forward, I needed to set up a new game plan.

One of the biggest parts of this process was understanding that one of the coping mechanisms I had created for myself was creating different personas to step into in different situations. Through this process I identified three different personas. There was public Bronwen, private Bronwen and then there was party Bronwen (or Bronweena as she was known!) These three personas had completely different characteristics, which meant that I became a different person in different situations. I even had different signatures for two of them.

Maintaining these three personas was exhausting. Trying to remember who I was supposed to be at different times was exhausting. When you overlay my underlying characteristic of perfection and then overlay again with the total suppression of emotion it's relatively easy to see why something had to give and I experienced a total implosion.

Looking at it now, my comfort zone was very rarely anything but comfortable! My life was a slog. I didn't sleep well, I dragged myself out of bed, I was sluggish, exhausted and desperately unhappy.

Having worked out what I want in my comfort zone, I now align what I want with speaking my truth. If what I want aligns with my values then I add the thing, person, activity whatever to my comfort zone.

I'm a big believer in the knowledge we have within ourselves. I believe that our answers always come from within, so I've become an advocate for listening to the messages that pop into our heads during the day, seemingly out of nowhere. One of the messages I receive constantly is the importance of speaking *your* truth.

I'm a highly visual person and often receive my 'forehead slap city' moments after seeing an image, a quote or a passage of text. For those of you who are also visual, this is how I visualise 'speaking my truth'.

Imagine that you're there when King Arthur pulls Excalibur from the stone. You watch as he places his hands around the hilt and then confidently pulls his destiny out of the stone. Right next to his stone is another stone with another sword. It's your turn to place your hands around the hilt of the sword and confidently pull your destiny towards you. This sword is your sword of truth. You extract it, hold it triumphantly above your head and then you plunge it into the ground and stand next to it.

This picture becomes your beacon. Any time you are wondering what your truth is, picture yourself standing next to your sword and then picture yourself speaking your truth in that moment.

This visualisation was so powerful for me because I'd never stood in my own truth before. I had lived my life in a zone of chasing other people's dreams, being everything to everyone and never putting myself first. This visualisation is a simple, elegant process that helps me shut out the noise of a situation and get straight to the heart of a matter. It helps me sort through my 'stuff' and work out where my truth lies.

A lot of people will tell you that to get out of your comfort zone you have to make uncomfortable choices. I've heard it said that you should do something uncomfortable every day to help you eliminate your fears, and to experience rapid growth in your life. I like to view this a bit differently, because to me doing something uncomfortable everyday sounds like introducing more struggle into our lives. I don't know about you, but I've certainly had more than enough struggle in my life without adding any more.

My suggestion is to explore what we can do to expand horizons in a way that is kind and supports our growing and developing without stress, fear and struggle. What if we simply take a step back and acknowledge that the comfort zone we've created for ourselves is not really comfortable? In fact, let's go to our sword of truth, stand in non-judgemental honesty about this matter and acknowledge that our comfort zone contains a lot of really, really uncomfortable things. The daily grind. The struggle of toxic people. Jobs we hate. Situations that clash with our values and grind us down until there's nothing left. I'm sure you can immediately name at least half a dozen more that are relevant to your life.

Then, let's stand up and visualise where our comfort zone is on the ground around us. Within that space are all the really, really uncomfortable things. Outside that space are a host of amazing, fabulous, fantastic and fun things. Things we really want in our lives. Hopes, dreams, laughter, joy. Now make a conscious decision about where you want to stand. Inside or outside the comfort zone you've drawn around you on the floor? Take a step outside the invisible line of the zone you've created and feel what it feels like to stand in all the things you want.

If we view this as making an uncomfortable choice every day, it becomes something we have to force ourselves to do from a place of fear. I don't know about you, but I just don't always feel courageous, so I prefer to suggest that you make a list of things you really, really want. Make the list as long as you want, as wide and varied as you want, full of simple, tiny, small, medium and big things. Don't be shy – it's just some words on a piece of paper – nothing harmful in that! Then each day read through your list and picture yourself stepping outside the invisible line to get one of those things. Feel the relief at moving to a space full of love, laughter, fun and fabulous, fantastic things. When you view it like this, it becomes a bit of fun – something that you can do no matter how you feel.

Courage and discipline are words that are bandied around as being the source of great achievements. I agree that sometimes in our lives courage and discipline are required in large quantities. But I believe that in our day-to-day lives if we just break our 'stuff' down into small chunks that we can tackle one step at a time, then it's much easier for us to set our priorities and tick them off one at a time.

When we approach things in a simple way and have small, easily achievable tasks, courage and discipline aren't required anywhere near as often. Life becomes simple, and more importantly, life becomes about simple steps that make us happy.

 KISSdoms

1. Write down three things you would love to do, achieve, see – you get the idea.
2. Put this list in order of importance.

_____
_____
_____
_____
_____
_____
_____
_____
_____
_____

3. Taking each item on the list, write down three simple things you can do to work towards achieving this item.

_____
_____
_____
_____
_____
_____
_____
_____
_____
_____
_____
_____

4. Starting with the first item on the list, focus on completing the three simple things until you have achieved the item.

_____
_____
_____
_____
_____
_____
_____
_____
_____

5. Move on to the next item on the list.

_____
_____
_____
_____
_____
_____
_____
_____
_____
_____
_____
_____

Notes

CHAPTER 12

"Music can reach those places where words alone cannot go"

(Ellen Synakowski)

Magic

Take a moment to pause and remember the last time you stopped and looked at something in absolute awe. We see the expressions on the faces of young children who find delight and joy in everything around them. Can you remember the feeling of your eyes widening as your thoughts catch up to what you've seen? Your mind runs wild with all the possibilities that this new information brings into your world.

One of the resources I came across during my recovery was a relatively new theory called 'Shadow Work', by Alyce Barry.

The theory of shadow work says that we are each born into a '360 degree personality'. As young children we live all the aspects of our personality, without editing or censoring. As we grow up, however, our social conditioning teaches us that certain parts of our personality are unacceptable to the people around us, so we learn to repress those slices of our personality. I believe that the more of ourselves we repress, the more the magic leaves our lives. By the time we're about seven years old, the way we've interpreted the messages we've received through our social conditioning will significantly influence the way we approach our lives moving forwards.

Have you ever heard or used the expression '…they were behaving like big kids'? As adults we're supposed to behave in a particular way. As children, we're completely innocent to the world around us until we're forced to grow up. Society tells us that after a certain age we're supposed to be mature, and child-like behaviour is no longer appropriate. Whilst I agree that there are some aspects of life that we do need to adopt to be able to become self-sufficient,

I'm not sure that we need to lose all our child-like characteristics. In fact, I would argue that losing some of them negatively impacts our lives and makes us more susceptible to media and marketing messaging.

Until I was forced to stop, I hadn't realised that my life was completely devoid of magic. In supressing my emotion, I had also completely repressed my ability to recognise and experience the magic of my life. Why is it that as adults we complicate our lives to the extent that we just 'have to get away' or 'have to take a break' for us to survive? It's almost as though if we can take a quick break from the struggle then it will all be okay to come back to.

We don't ever stop to question where our lives are at, or why we're so unhappy or under so much stress that we have to have a break to survive. We simply - blindly - accept that this is our lot in life, it's what we have to do because 'life wasn't meant to be easy'. We've been fed the message that 'someone out there is worse off than I am so I should be grateful' and we turn that into the reason why where we're at is okay. We're slowly killing ourselves or pointing ourselves directly on a collision course with chaos, simply because we don't stop to recognise that there is another way.

When we go to places like Las Vegas and Disneyland, we're in our element and we can relax and have a great time. We get carried away by the magic that surrounds us. Why do we behave so differently in these places? Because it's expected of us. It's totally acceptable to laugh, let go, be big children, to immerse ourselves in magic and fun and laughter. We're transported to another world where the troubles of our lives don't exist in that short period of time. You can run through the streets of Disneyland and no one will look at you strangely. You can wear a badge that says 'Happy Birthday' and everyone will celebrate with you all day. No matter who you are, you're special and the whole focus and atmosphere of the world around you is to make sure everyone has an absolutely awesome day.

Why aren't we expected to have magic, fun and laughter in our everyday lives? Why is it only okay for us to live this way in short periods of time, when we visit specific places? Why has our social conditioning moved to such an extreme that the messaging we receive is all about hard work, responsibility and the everyday slog? Why do we have to be ready with an excuse as to why we have something, want something, go somewhere or do something differently to others? Why do we have to have an excuse ready for why someone else is doing something – 'you can afford that becaus...'? Why? Why? Why?

Magic comes into our lives in lots of different ways. One of the things I love about technology advances in our phones is that we now have the ability to snapshot our moments from the palm of our hands. They say a picture is worth a thousand words and we can now capture the best moments of our lives wherever we are. I love that I can take photos with my phone, that it automatically syncs the photos to my computer and the screen saver on my computer scrolls through the photos throughout the day and I can catch glimpses of special moments and relive the feelings at different times during the day.

One of the hidden ways magic comes into our lives is through music. For a small portion of us, music is something that we are exposed to in our youth. Some of us are exposed to music through our parents, either through their listening to the radio or playing CD's or playing music from the computer. Others like me are luckier still to have had a music program at school where we were immersed in different instruments and have the opportunity to actually create the music ourselves. Almost all of us have no idea of the effect that music actually has on us, and the powerful, ability that music has to influence our minds, our energy and our flow in life. Never underestimate the magic of listening to your favourite music on full blast while dancing around the house like an idiot!

If combining our thoughts, feelings and words with the power of music can influence what happens in our life, then it seems to me to be extremely important that we're really conscious of how those things exist in our life.

Music is so powerful and on the whole we are so unaware of its impact on us. Worldwide there are fans of celebrity artists who fall in love with the music that is produced. How many people stop to consider where the music has come from? How have the lyrics come to be written? What is the artists' connection to the music? In most cases, songs with an upbeat tempo that are catchy and get your feet and head (and sometimes even your body!) moving along connect with people in droves.

But have you ever stopped to consider what you're singing when you sing along to these songs? In most cases, most people aren't consciously connecting with the lyrics they are singing. The artist has a connection to the song that has usually come from an emotional connection of some sort – be it painful, heartfelt, happy, sad and so on. Their connection with the song is what actually sells it to us as good. But if we then start singing these lyrics, we start connecting with the emotion of the song and we start telling the story of the song.

If combining our thoughts, feelings and words with the power of music can influence what happens in our life, then it seems to me to be extremely important that we're really conscious of how those things exist in our life. Music calls to us because it connects us to different aspects of our lives. By becoming conscious of the power that music can have in your life, you can become more conscious about how different music affects you. This means you can have more control over the way that advertising, movies and music affects you and you can become more conscious about decisions you are making for your life rather than responding in a pre-programmed way.

When you simplify everything down to one step at a time, you take the panic out of everything you do. It becomes easy to walk outside, take a deep breath and revel in the fresh air and brilliant blue sky that surrounds you. Or, it might be walking outside, taking a deep breath and experiencing the fierce energy in a storm that's raging. Reconnecting with the small things that bring the energy within us buzzing to life is a very simple but highly effective way to bring magic into our lives. Close your eyes, stand outside, breathe in the air and take notice of how you're feeling. Feel the energy shift within you and then open your eyes and see where your thoughts take you.

Go for a walk at the beach, along a river, or through a nature trail and breathe in the air around you. Open your eyes and find the things that resonate with you and let them feed the energy within.

One of the exercises that my counsellor asked me to complete was to go into nature and find a symbol that connected me with the earth and could provide me with a reminder I could turn to in times of chaos. I chose to bring her a rose from my garden. The rose is the most stunning red colour and it has the most beautiful fragrance. The rose is called 'Courage' and just seeing it reminds me that all I need to do in any situation is to gather the courage to take one step at a time.

Have you ever heard the phrase... *don't forget to stop and smell the roses?* We're all connected to nature; we've just forgotten it somewhere along the way. This exercise was one of the most powerful on my recovery road. Taking the time to find a connection with nature shifted my thoughts, and I now often find myself stopped by the smell of fresh herbs, or I notice beautiful flowers in gardens as we drive by, or I notice the birds playing in the trees in the garden. I notice the small things in my life and I have time to stop and appreciate them. Most importantly, all I have to do is look out my back windows and see my 'Courage' rose bush and it helps me to easily shift my thoughts into a different track. Shifting your thoughts, even slightly, means you can see things differently. Once you see things differently it opens up a world of possibilities. A world of possibilities means you can quit the struggle, and quitting the struggle makes it much easier to move forward.

 KISSdoms

1. Find three pieces of music/songs from three different music genres - for example, you might choose a piece of music from pop/rock, blues and classical genres.

2. Play each piece of music in turn and write down how each piece of music makes you feel, noting your body's response, your mood, the way your blood moves through your veins and where your thoughts go.

3. Consciously acknowledge the impact that the different types of music have on you.

4. Use this knowledge to help you be more conscious of situations where music can trigger pre-programmed responses.

_____
_____
_____
_____
_____
_____
_____
_____
_____

Notes

CHAPTER 13

*"Take nothing on its looks;
take everything on evidence.
There's no better rule."*

(Charles Dickens – Great Expectations)

No is a Complete Sentence!

Often we find ourselves constrained by 'rules' that we don't even know exist, that aren't actually written anywhere but are drummed into us as part of our social conditioning as a child. We are taught from a very young age what behaviour is acceptable and which parts of our character must remain hidden from the world for us to be accepted.

I believe that at heart we are all born with kind, generous and loving souls – it is only once we're exposed to the world around us that greed, fear and a relentless search for more are introduced to us.

Throughout our history as a species rules have been used by all different manner of groups and organisations to control the behaviour of their members, and to further increase the hold of power of those at the top of the group or organisation. History tells us that it's the victor who writes the story of what happened during the battle; however, the rules that were broken to win the battle are very rarely documented. Why? Because if everyday people realised that rules can be broken then power and control over them would be lost.

To some extent, rules are needed to assist in keeping people safe. Can you imagine if there were no road rules and it was fine to drive as fast as you like, change lanes without indicating, drive under the influence of drugs and alcohol and pay no heed to killing anyone? Some rules in our lives are necessary for the greater good. Unfortunately, most of us have never learned that there are some rules that we can break free of for our own greater good.

For example, how many times have you said 'Yes' to doing something when you really didn't want to do it, and in fact, it was detrimental to you to have said 'Yes'?

Learning to say 'No' to things, people, groups and events and so on. that really don't serve you well is one of the most empowering things you can ever do for yourself.

Being a perfectionist, I found myself trying to be everything to everyone and feeling like I failed every single time. I never put myself first, I never considered what I needed to be okay, and I never stopped to work out whether what I was doing was detrimental to my own health.

Not once did I stop to question what working in that soul-crushing industry was doing to me, physically, psychologically and spiritually. I was caught up in the system, and felt compelled to continue on when what I really needed to do was say 'NO! – this isn't working for me' and step away to a career that matched my values. Instead, I worked for seventeen years in situations that clashed with my personal values. I told myself I was working to help others to make their dreams come true, and slogging from the inside to try and make changes to an industry driven by façades, greed and fear and with products that were mostly beneficial to the organisation who provided them.

We often create a version of ourselves that we believe is the most acceptable to those around us. One of the most liberating moments of my life came not long after I was in pieces on the floor and I couldn't get back up again. My counsellor gave me the tools to realise that if I took the time to examine each piece I could _choose_ whether I picked it up again and made it a part of me, or whether that piece no longer served me well and I could thank it for its contribution and let it go. When you are able to say 'No' to pieces of yourself that you no longer need moving forwards, you can say 'No' to anything.

Choosing to put yourself first, and saying 'No' to others is perhaps the biggest hurdle in our lives.

I can't count the number of times I've heard people say 'I really didn't feel like I could say "No". We find ourselves in time-poor situations of high stress, simply because we said 'Yes' when we should have said 'No''.

I have missed weddings, birthdays, social and special occasions over the years simply because I was a 'Yes' person and didn't ever stop to consider whether it was something I wanted, or indeed even needed to do.

I've found myself alone in hotel rooms around the world whilst important celebrations are happening at home simply because I was a 'Yes' person and didn't ever stop to consider whether what I was doing was important enough to outweigh the cost of what I was missing.

With the value of hindsight and the ability to look back on my life, I can tell you with my hand on my heart that there was not one single thing that I was doing for work that was more

important than the events I missed out on. I was a 'go-to' person simply because I always made myself available to sort out everyone else's problems.

Don't get me wrong – I was VERY good at my job. I was VERY good at solving problems and I was VERY good at keeping everyone happy. The only person suffering through this situation was me and it wasn't until I was on the floor and couldn't get up again that I realised that I had been miserable for almost my entire life. I had very few real connections in my life and I felt like I flitted around the edges of my friends and family.

> *Learning to say 'No' has been the single most freeing exercise in my life to date. Removing guilt and obligation from my play book and refusing to bow to the ingrained conditioning that says that I must serve everyone else at the exclusion of myself has allowed me to create a life where I can choose to participate in those things that are kind to me.*

That doesn't mean that I don't ever do anything for anyone else – it simply means that I choose the things I want to do, and make sure that there is time in my life to make choices for myself as well. I make sure that there is time in every day allocated for exercise and meditation. I make sure that there is time allocated in every day for me to spend time creating healthy and nutritious food. I make sure there is time allocated in every week for real connections with my family and friends. These are my non-negotiables. <u>Everything</u> else is optional, and open for negotiation.

One of the greatest pieces of wisdom I can share with you is this: **'No' is a complete sentence.** Saying 'No' is enough. We're programmed to be so helpful to others that it is excruciating when we have to say 'No'. To ease the pain of this experience we attempt to explain to others why we have been forced to say 'No'. We work to make the story as convincing as possible to make sure that the 'No' is accepted by the other person.

I am here to tell you that if you can get comfortable with saying 'No' then that is all that is needed. I encourage you to try and say 'No' to things at least three times a day. And when you say 'No', leave the 'No' as a complete sentence and see how often someone actually asks you for an explanation. I am willing to bet that there will be very few occasions when you are asked for any further information.

If you are like I was, and you are a serial 'Yes' person, I can promise you that the first time you say 'No' it will be really, really, really, really uncomfortable for you. You may even spend days afterwards worrying about whether you've done the right thing saying 'No', and you will be tempted to contact the person you said 'No' to and explain to them that there is now a way that you can say 'Yes'. Fight this instinct with everything within you – it's the first step to breaking your 'Yes' habit, and fighting this instinct will help to silence the voice within that is telling you you've made the wrong decision.

The second time you say 'No', it will be really, really, really uncomfortable but not quite as uncomfortable as the first time. Eventually, saying 'No' will be comfortable and you will be confident that when you do say 'Yes' it will be because it's something you want to be involved in, or doing.

Get used to 'No' being a complete sentence and watch how your world opens up.

KISSdoms

1. Saying 'No' really comes down to practice – the more you do it, the easier it becomes.

2. Write down three areas of your life where you say 'Yes' to things when you really don't want to.

3. Memorise this list until you know it by heart.

4. The next time you are asked to do something from this list:
   - STOP
   - Take a deep breath
   - Say 'No'

5. Practice saying 'No' to these three things until it becomes easy.

   _____
   _____
   _____
   _____
   _____
   _____
   _____
   _____

6. Once you become comfortable with saying 'No' it will be easier to say it in other areas of your life.

   _____
   _____
   _____
   _____
   _____
   _____
   _____
   _____
   _____

Notes

CHAPTER 14

"Everything changed the day she figured out there was exactly enough time for the important things in her life"

(Brian Andreas)

Keep It Super Simple

Conclusion

Do you remember when you were a child, and your parents tried to get you to eat things that you hadn't tried before? Usually, the immediate reaction was to say "Yuck – I don't like that!" and you would fight tooth and nail to be allowed to stick to the food you were comfortable with and you knew was 'safe'. You would most likely then enter into a negotiation where your parents would try to coax, cajole and sometimes even bribe you to be adventurous and try something new. Sometimes you'd give in and sometimes you'd find new things you liked.

I remember roaming the countryside and revelling in all that nature offered – walking or horse-riding bush trails or at the beach – and breathing in the fresh air. I also remember playing as a child – where make-believe and imagination were the only ingredients necessary for a good time, or riding bikes to the local school to engage in a highly competitive tennis match amongst friends. Freedom reigned and laughter and sunshine shone through our days.

Then we got older, and our social conditioning taught us that our simple life was no longer enough. We were taught that make-believe and imagination were no longer appropriate. We were told it was time to grow up and take life more seriously. We joined the migration and drive to success and we forgot that laughter makes the world go around. We became serious about our lives, our world and our futures. We pushed ourselves beyond our limits in our quest for success – and we told ourselves it was so we'd be set up for our future. But at what cost?

When do we know we have enough? When can we stop and relax and no longer have to slog our way through our lives? What is the point of a future full of sickness, depression and exhaustion?

There is no formal definition of success – yet we are all driven to achieve it, be it, obtain it, own it. If we don't know what it is, then how can we ever reach it? Our lives have become complicated and complex in our desperate scramble to achieve. We start to live in a world where we always need more. Our desperate need for more triggers our brains to believe there is not enough. If there is not enough, then that means we are in competition with everyone else for the limited amount that is available. Therefore life becomes about 'me against everyone else'. We can never win whilst our lives are set up in this fashion. There is always a loser in this scenario.

I believe it's time to reverse the trend. Let's stop, breathe and acknowledge that right here, right now, we have everything we need and we are okay. Let's simplify our lives and bring back the fun, laughter and imagination. It is these things that will drive our lives forward and truly connect us to happiness.

My life imploded in the space of minutes. My life shattered into a million pieces around me. I healed my life by consciously choosing which pieces to pick up again and which pieces to thank for their contribution so far but leave behind, as I would no longer need them.

In every situation, in every part of our lives, we have the choice to feel better or feel worse. Our greatest challenge is to find the space in our everyday activities to stop and consciously make this choice. My challenge to you is to choose the things you truly want in your life – the things that you love. Let's have more love and laughter and less stress and desperation.

KISSing is the process I've found that has helped me to heal my life and find a happier, lighter way to live. It has reduced the stress and exhaustion in my life and for the first time in a long time I sleep soundly at night.

It is my heartfelt hope that it can help you find your way as well. I choose to live my life differently. I choose to say 'No' when I need to. I choose to acknowledge that I'm not perfect and never will be.

My wish for you is best encapsulated in the words of an anonymous author:

'Be bold enough to use your voice, brave enough to listen to your heart, and strong enough to live the life you've always imagined'.

The choice is yours!

Contact Details

To book Bronwen Sciortino for a keynote presentation, half, full or two-day workshop nationally or internationally, please contact:

Bronwen Sciortino
sheIQ Life
PO Box 65
Melville, WA 6956

Ph: +61 438 624 868
E: info@sheiqlife.com
W: www.sheiqlife.com

References

I have been very privileged to access a host of resources that have helped shape the path that I now travel.

Following are a list of resources that have helped me put this book together:

- Gregg Braden — New York Times best-selling author and internationally renowned pioneer in bridging science, ancient wisdom and the real world. www.greggbraden.com
- Danielle LaPorte — Best-selling Canadian author, motivational speaker, entrepreneur, and blogger www.daniellelaporte.com
- Stephen Karpman — The drama triangle - psychological and social model of human interaction
- Susan Ariel Rainbow Kennedy (SARK) — American author & illustrator of self-help books. www.planetsark.com
- Michael Neill — Internationally renowned transformative coach and best-selling author www.supercoach.com
- Merriam-Webster Online Dictionary — www.merriam-webster.com
- Wikipedia — www.wikipedia.com
- Eleanor Roosevelt — Former First Lady of the United States of America
- Esther Hicks — American international speaker & author. www.abraham-hicks.com
- Mahatma Gandhi — Now deceased, Mahatma Gandhi was the pre-eminent leader of the Indian independence movement in British-ruled India
- Very Best Quotes — www.verybestquotes.com
- Leo Tolstoy — Now deceased, Leo Tolstoy was a Russian novelist, short story writer, essayist, playwright and philosopher who primarily wrote novels and short stories.
- Dictionary.com — www.dictionary.com
- Todd Hermann — Visionary leader in the sporting world who focuses on 'helping players get out of their own way so they can reach their true potential'. www.thepeakathlete.com
- Iain Thomas — Best-selling author
- Henry Ford — American industrialist, the founder of the Ford Motor Company and sponsor of the development of the assembly line technique of mass production.
- Seung Sahn — South Korea Jogye Seon master and founder of the international Kwan Um School of Zen - the largest Zen institution present in the western hemisphere.
- Neale Donald Walsch — American author of the series Conversations with God. www.nealedonaldwalsch.com
- Ellen Synakowski — Connection practice, trainer and coach. www.ellensynakowski.com
- Alyce Barry — Shadow work. www.alycebarry.com
- Charles Dickens — English writer and social critic who created some of the world's best-known financial characters and is regarded as the greatest novelist of the Victorian era.
- Brian Andreas — American writer, painter, sculptor, technologist and publisher widely known for an ongoing series of works presented by the author as Story People. www.storypeople.com

I am grateful for the wisdom and knowledge that each and every one of these resources has brought to my life and my writing.

Thank you

This book, and my recovery in general, would not have been possible without the love, encouragement and support of a number of significant people.

- Jon Sciortino – my number 1 supporter – your unfailing belief in me has sustained me throughout my recovery and has given me the strength to keep moving forwards when others have doubted the value of my work.

- Helen Parsons – you've always been there, quietly giving me love and support. You've influenced my life in so many ways. I will always be grateful.

- Ted Parsons – every little girl needs a hero – you were, and always will be mine.

- Nairn Walker – you challenge my thinking and make sure I don't get stuck in old, self-limiting patterns and beliefs. You've been such an inspiration to me and I'm so glad our paths are aligned.

- Jocelyn Parsons – when I was in a million pieces and couldn't get back up you were there and encouraged me to start taking steps back into life again.

- Karen & Andre Clay, Catherine Rapley, Sharon Marsden and John & Lynne Rogerson – a girl could not ask for better friends. No matter that we may be separated by distance at times, your ongoing love and support of me played a massive part in my recovery.

- Melaney Ryan, Margaret Turner and Paul Ryan – my spiritual, energy and psychological team. . I am honoured to have walked this path with you and for the guidance, wisdom and experience you so freely shared with me.

- Robyn Henderson – your writing system, editing skills and ongoing encouragement kept me focused and moving forwards during the writing and publishing process. I will always be grateful for the ability to access your wisdom and experience.

- Kelsey Allen – my typesetter and friend – your enthusiasm and excitement at the publishing of my first book will always be remembered!

- Dale Simmonds – for my illustrations – I love that you connected with the essence of the book. Your talent is undeniable. I will forever by proud of the end result and cannot thank you enough for your contribution.

- Janelle Dix – my printer – many thanks for holding my hand through the printing process – your assistance was much appreciated.

I am extremely lucky to be surrounded by such exceptional people who enrich my life both personally and professionally every day.

There are a number of other people whose lives have touched mine both over the years and during my recovery. My heartfelt thanks to you all and for the role that you have played in my life. Much love and a multitude of thanks to you all.

Notes

I'm exhausted! Life wasn't meant to be easy! I need a break!

Most of us trudge through our lives believing that we have no control over what happens to us, and that we must make the 'best of our lot'.

Society teaches us we can have everything we want – but it comes at a price.

Our world has gone crazy! There's no formal definition of success – yet we're all driven to achieve it; be it; obtain it; own it. And we get there by being everything, to everyone all whilst being the busiest person on the planet. How do we know when we have enough?

We take on the world – but we often end up leaving ourselves behind. Our lives are so complex when simplicity will do. As children we're taught what's right, wrong, acceptable and unacceptable by our families, friends, schools, communities and the world at large.

But what if they're wrong?

Inspiring individuals to live their lives by the mantra of Keep It Super Simple (KISS), Bronwen Sciortino leads you on a journey that challenges the status quo, raises consciousness and helps people to wake up to how different their lives can be. Combining simplicity and wisdom (KISSdom), laughter, tears and simple steps for changing your way forward, Bronwen will change the way you look at your life, and how you choose to live every day.

You will be inspired to step outside the norm and reverse the current life trends, simplify your life and find ways to bring back the fun, laughter and imagination that has vanished over time.

www.ingramcontent.com/pod-product-compliance
Lightning Source LLC
Chambersburg PA
CBHW050435010526
44118CB00013B/1539